APPLE WATCH SERIES 9 USER GUIDE

The Complete Manual For Beginners & Seniors With Instructions On How To Master The New Apple Watch Series 9. With Illustrations & WatchOS 10 Tips & Tricks

By

Alan McDonald

© **Copyright 2023 Alan McDonald**

All rights reserved. No part of this book shall be reproduced, stored in a retrieval system, or transmitted by any means, electronic, mechanical, photocopying, recording, or otherwise, without written permission from the publisher. Although every precaution has been taken in the preparation of this book, the publisher and author assume no responsibility for errors or omissions. Nor is any liability assumed for damages resulting from the use of the information contained herein.

Table of Contents

INTRODUCTION 1
CHAPTER ONE 5
HOW TO CONFIGURE & PAIR WATCH WITH IPHONES 5
   How To Wake & Configure Your Watch 5
   Turn On The Mobile Service 7
   Connect Several Watches To Your iPhone 8
   Change To A New Watch 9
  Applications For Watch 11
   Fire Up The Watch Software 11
   Get The Lowdown On The Watch 13
  Put The Watch On Charge 13
   Prepare The Battery Pack 13
   Get Started With Watch Charging 13
  Activate & Deactivate Your Watch 19
   Always On 20
   Awaken To Your Last Task 23
  Secure Or Unlock The Watch 24
   Open Watch 24
   Set A New Passcode 25
   Immediately Secure Lock 26

Switch To Other Language / Country 29
Flip Your Wrists Digital Crown 30
CHAPTER TWO 33
HOW TO SET UP A RELATIVE'S WATCH 33
Set Up Watch For A Relative 34
Use The School Time Watch App 40
Schedule Classes 40
Get Health And Activity Reports 43
Spend Apple Cash With Family 47
Family Members May Manage Apple Pay 48
CHAPTER THREE 50
HOW TO USE WATCH APPLICATIONS 50
Launch Software By Touching 51
Start A Program From The Dock 52
Alter Programs Shown In The Dock 53
Watch App Management 55
Place Your Programs In A Grid Format 55
Watch Allows You To Check The Time 57
Make Use Of Watch App, "Focus" 59
Focus On/Off Toggle 59
Prepare Yourself To Focus 61

Alter the Watch's Visuals & Typeface 63
    Alter Volume 64
    The Haptic Alerts Switch 65
    Toggle The Haptic Feedback 66
    Tape In The Time 67
CHAPTER FOUR 69
HOW TO CHECK YOUR WATCH FOR ALERTS .. 69
    Reply A Message Sent To You 69
    See Your Unread Messages 70
    Modify Watch Alert Settings 72
    Choose Which Applications Notify You 73
    A Medium To Modify Alert Settings 74
    Adjust Your Apple Id Preferences 77
    Adjust Your Address & Phone Number 77
    Speed Up Your Watch Experience Using Shortcuts 81
CHAPTER FIVE 83
HOW TO SET UP HANDWASHING 83
    To activate Handwashing 83
Join A Wireless Internet Connection 85
    Choose A Wireless Network 85
Communicate With External Audio Devices 87

Plug In Your Wireless Headphones 87
The Watch Is A Handy Tool For Passing Off Responsibilities...90
Use Your Watch As A Password...................... 91
Switch On Auto-Unlock 92
Use Watch To Unlock Your iPhone 93
Put Watch To Use Without An iPhone 94
Connect Your Watch To A Cellular Service 97
Upgrade Your Mobile Plan 97
Control The On/Off Status Of Your Phone.....98

CHAPTER SIX 100
WATCH'S SECURITY FEATURES 100
See & Manage Your Medical Id Card............ 101
Watch's Fall Detection Can Be Controlled.... 105
Control Watch's Collision Detection System 107
Activating Voiceover On Your Watch 109
Adjust The Volume Of The Voiceover........... 109
Gestures Used With The Voiceover System.. 110
The Voiceover Dial.. 111
Alter Voiceover's Preferences 112
Use Voiceover To Set Up Your Watch 113
Set Up Your Watch 114

Use Your iPhone To Manage Your Watch 116
Manage Adjacent Electronics 117
Watch's Assistive Touch Feature....................... 118
Connect Assistive touch 119
Assistive touch With The Watch.................... 119
Use The Pointer In Motion 121
Modify Your Assistive Touch Options 123
Zoom In On Your Watch................................ 124
CHAPTER SEVEN 128
CUSTOMIZE THE SIZE OF TEXT 128
Modify The Font Size.................................... 128
Modify The Layout Of Text........................... 128
Set Up And Use RTT On The Watch............. 130
Set Watch For Accessible Listening............... 132
Altering Airpods' Preferences 133
Playback Of Homepod Transcripts............... 134
Activate Watch's Accessibility Functions...... 134
The Watch Accessibility Shortcut 135
Restart Your Watch 136
Discard Watch 137
Recover A Watch From A Previous Backup.. 139

Software Updates Your Watch 140
CHAPTER EIGHT 142
HOW TO MONITOR YOUR BLOOD OXYGEN LEVELS 142
See And Modify Your Schedule 145
Alter Your Perspective On Recent Occurrences 146
Inquire On A Friend's Whereabouts 151
Check In With Your Pals 153
Find Your Way, Or Reach Out To A Buddy .. 154
Talk To A Close Pal 155
Track Lost Gadgets 155
Track Down An Airtag Or Other Object 161
Use Your Watch To Monitor Your Pulse 165
Medications May Be Tracked On Watch 167
Use Mindfulness With Your Watch 171
Enjoy Guided Meditations 175
Choose A Picture Album 177
Pick The Album For Watch 178
Examine Snapshots & Recollections 181
Have A Look At The Forecast 184
Modify The Weather Recordings 186

Set & React To Reminders................................. 187
   Check Your Notes For Upcoming Events 188
   Set An Alarm To Remind Yourself................. 190
   Modify A Prompt 191
Explore New Areas 193
   Find A Close-By Provider 194
   View & Investigate The Immediate Area 195
   Place & Reposition Map Markers 197
   Find Your Way... 198
CHAPTER NINE 204
HOW TO USE YOUR WATCH TO TAKE CALLS 204
   Respond To A Call 204
   Watch With Dual-SIM Capability.................. 210
   Schedule Checks & Edits With Watch 212
      Examine Watch For Upcoming Events......... 213
      Get Moving With Your Device 214
      Adapt Your Perspective 216
      Examine Months And Years 217
Get Your Apple Fitness+ Routine Going 221
   Get Moving With An Apple TV Exercise....... 221
   Summing Up A Workout 223

Use Shareplay For A Group Workout................224
   Create A Group Workout On Your iPhone ...225
   Launch The Fitness App 226
   Participate In A Group Workout....................227
Alter The Visuals In Fitness+ Programs 228
   Modify The Displayed Statistics 229
   Feed In Subtitles And Captions 231

INTRODUCTION

The Apple Watch Series 9, which debuted in September 2023 and succeeded the Apple Watch Series 9, is the newest version of the Apple Watch, which was first released in 2015.

The new S9 SiP boosts speed and capabilities on Apple Watch Series 9, and the watch also has a new double-tap gesture, a brighter display, quicker on-device Siri with access to and logging of health data, Precision Finding for iPhone, and more. The Series 9 Apple Watch is powered by watchOS 10, which includes reimagined applications, a Smart Stack, new watch faces, cycling and hiking enhancements, and mental health resources.

As a major step toward Apple 2030, the company's goal of becoming carbon neutral throughout its entire business, manufacturing supply chain, and product life cycle by 2030, consumers may now choose a carbon neutral option when purchasing any Apple Watch.

The new Apple Watch collection is now available for preorder, and will begin shipping on Friday, September 22.

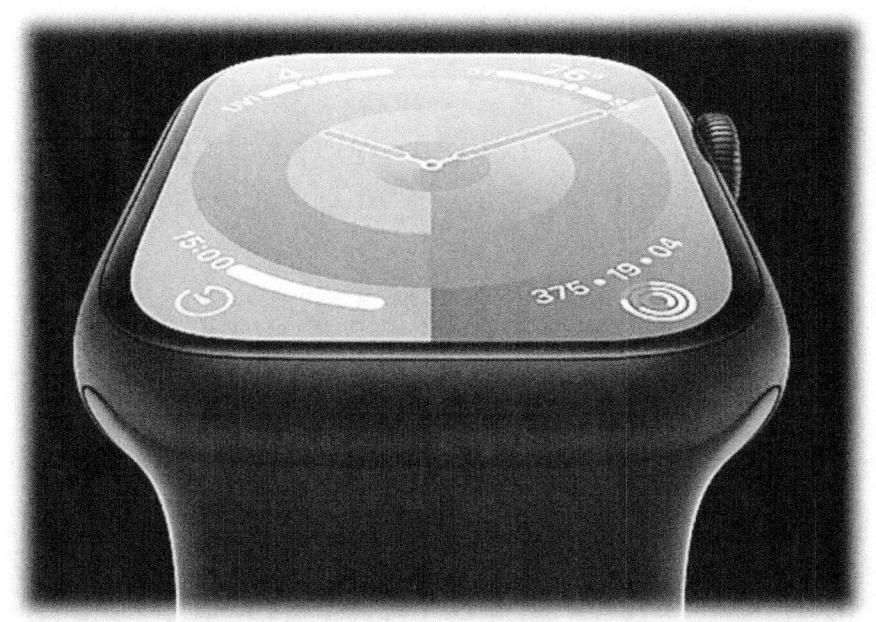

With strong new features to improve users' health, fitness, communications, and safety, Apple Watch Series 9 is an even more necessary companion than ever.

The Apple Watch is an "indispensible companion" that improves the health, fitness, communication, and safety of millions of people. The new double-tap gesture, brighter display, and in-device Siri are just a few of the many innovations we're delivering with our most advanced Apple Watch portfolio to date, which also includes our first carbon neutral goods. There has never been a more compelling opportunity to experience Apple Watch, whether people are upgrading from prior models or purchasing their first.

Apple's first carbon neutral goods are Apple Watch Series 9 models with certain casing and band configurations.

The S9 SiP, exclusive to the Apple Watch Series 9, is a custom-designed piece of Apple silicon. The Apple Watch Series 4 uses Apple's most powerful watch processor to date, bringing with it a slew of system-wide enhancements and brand-new features including a new double tap gesture and an in-watch version of Siri with safe access to and logging of health data. The new 4-core Neural Engine in Apple Watch Series 9 is twice as fast at machine learning tasks as the 2-core Neural Engine in Apple Watch Series 9. Apple Watch Series 9 is able to keep its 19-hour battery life because to the power efficiency of the S9 SiP.

CHAPTER ONE

HOW TO CONFIGURE & PAIR WATCH WITH IPHONES

To use a Watch with watchOS 9, you'll need the iPhone 9 or later running iOS 16. With the help of the setup assistants on both your iPhone and your watch, pairing and setting up your Watch could not be simpler.

If you have problems viewing the screen on your Watch or iPhone, you may use VoiceOver and Zoom to get help.

How To Wake & Configure Your Watch

1. Strap the Watch on your wrist. Adjusting the Watch's band size or switching to a different band will make it a better fit for your wrist.
2. To turn on your Apple Watch, just press and hold the side button until the Apple logo displays.
3. Wait for the pairing screen to display on your iPhone and watch, then tap Continue.
4. You may also choose Pair New Watch from inside the Watch app on your iPhone.

1. Select the "Set up for me" symbol on the watch.
2. Move your iPhone until the Watch appears in the Watch app's viewfinder. The two electronic devices go together well.
3. Select Setup Watch, then follow the on-screen instructions on your iPhone and Watch to finish the setup.

While your Watch is syncing, you may tap Get to Know Your Watch to discover more about its features. This user guide, as well as the latest news and information on Watch, are all accessible from your iPhone. You may get this data by opening the Watch app on your iPhone and selecting Explore once you have set up your Watch.

Two Apple products, an iPhone and a watch are placed next to one another. You may see "Watch is Syncing" on your iPhone screen. There's a sync indicator on the Watch.

Turn On The Mobile Service

Cellular connection may be enabled on your Watch during the setup process. The Watch app on your iPhone will allow you to activate it at a later time if you change your mind.

Single network activation is required for both your iPhone and Watch. To complicate matters further, the iPhone you're using to set up the watch may have a different cellular operator than the watch itself.

Cellular networks aren't everywhere.

Pairing off?

- If you see a watch symbol while trying to link your device, it means that one of your iPhones is already connected to your Watch. You can't just restart your Watch without first wiping it clean.
- If the camera doesn't prompt pairing, here's what to do: Follow the on-screen instructions after selecting Pair Your Watch at the bottom of your iPhone's screen.

- In case your Apple Watch isn't able to sync with your iPhone, try these steps.

The watch must be unpaired.

1. Go to your iPhone's App Store and look for the Watch app.
2. Choose My Watch, and then hit All Watches at the very top of the screen.
3. Choose the Watch you want to de-pair by tapping the Info button next to it and then selecting Unpair Watch.

Connect Several Watches To Your iPhone

It's as simple as repeating the pairing process with your first Watch to add a second. Close the distance between your iPhone and your Watch, and when the connection screen for your Watch appears on your iPhone, hit Pair. Instead, you may do what I did:

1. Get out your iPhone and launch the Watch app.
2. Choose My Watch, and then touch All Watches in the menu that appears.
3. To add a watch, use the + button and carry out the on-screen prompts.

Change To A New Watch

While you're in range, your iPhone will automatically pair with any Watch you're wearing. Go to a different Watch and lift your wrist.

Or, you may choose your Watch:

1. Get out your iPhone and launch the Watch app.
2. Choose My Watch, and then touch All Watches in the menu that appears.
3. Cancel Auto Switch by pressing the off button.

Touch and hold the bottom of the watch screen slide up to activate Control Center, and then check for the connected status symbol to see whether your Watch is synced with your iPhone.

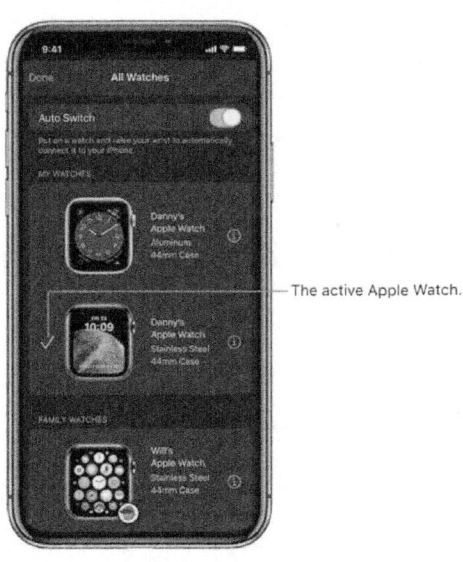
The active Apple Watch.

On the Watch app's All Watches screen, a tick denotes the currently active Watch.

Sync the Watch with a new iPhone.

To transfer your Watch from an older iPhone to a newer one, read on.

1. To backup your iPhone paired with your Watch, use iCloud Backup.
2. Learn how to activate your new iPhone. On the Apps & Data tab, pick Restore from an iCloud Backup to download and install the latest backup.
3. Complete iPhone setup and link your Watch with your new iPhone when prompted.

After setting up an iPhone, you'll get a notification on your Watch asking you to pair it. When prompted, enter your Watch's passcode after tapping OK.

Use your current iPhone or iPad cellular plan on your new Watch

If you already have a cellular Watch and want to switch to another Watch, you may use your current cellular plan by following these instructions:

1. Just launch the Watch app on your iPhone while wearing your Watch.
2. Choose "My Watch," then "Cellular," and finally "Info" next to your cellular plan.
3. Choose the carrier from the list, and then tap Delete Plan.

   Remove this Watch from your cellular plan by contacting your service provider.

4. Put on your newer Watch that supports cellular, take off your old watch, go to My Watch, and then hit Cellular.

   To enable cellular functionality on your watch, just follow the on-screen prompts.

Applications For Watch

If you have an iPhone, you can use the Watch app to change the watch face, tweak the settings and alerts, set up the Dock, and even install new applications directly from your wrist.

Fire Up The Watch Software

1. Choose Watch from the iPhone's app drawer.
2. To access your Watch's settings, choose My Watch.

If more than one Watch is synced with your iPhone, the settings for the currently selected Watch will be shown.

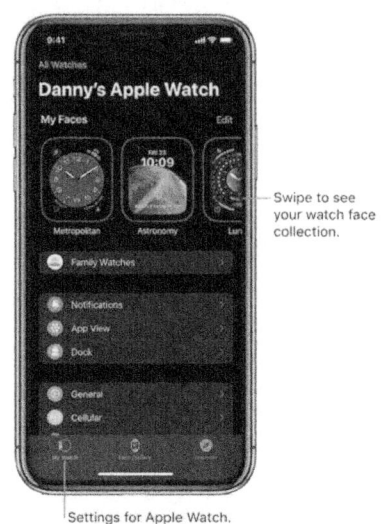

Settings for Apple Watch.

When you launch the Watch app on your iPhone, you'll be taken to the My Watch screen, which displays your watch faces and other personalization options. The Watch app has three tabs at the bottom of the screen: My Watch, where you can access Watch settings; Face Gallery, where you can browse various watch faces and complexities; and Explore, where you can read more about Watch.

Get The Lowdown On The Watch

Watch tips, an informative overview of your Watch, and this user guide can all be accessed via the iPhone app's Explore page.

Put The Watch On Charge

Prepare The Battery Pack

1. Put your charger or charging wire on a level table in a well-ventilated environment.

Either the Watch Magnetic Fast Charger to USB-C Cable (for Series 7 and Series 9) or the Watch Magnetic Charging Cable will be included with your Watch purchase (other models). Magnetic charging docks for the Watch or a MagSafe Dual USB adapter are also acceptable alternatives (sold separately).

2. Connect the charger to the power source (sold separately).
3. To use, connect the adapter to a working power source.

Rapid charging is not yet accessible everywhere.

Get Started With Watch Charging

For Watch Series 7 and above, use the Watch Magnetic Fast Charger; for Series 1–6, use the Watch Magnetic Charging Cable (USB-A end). A concave charging cord end magnetically sticks to the Watch's rear when charging.

Once charging begins, the Watch makes a noise and displays a charging sign, unless in quiet mode. The Watch's symbol turns red when the battery is low and green while charging. Watch charging icon becomes yellow in Low Power Mode.

Your Watch may be charged flat, on its side, or with the band open.

- Put your Watch on the dock if you're using the Watch Magnetic Charging Dock or the Watch MagSafe Dual Charger.
- If your battery is critically low, your screen may display a charging cable and a picture of the Watch Magnetic Quick Charger to USB-C Cable or Watch Magnetic Charging Cable.

Series 9 Watch

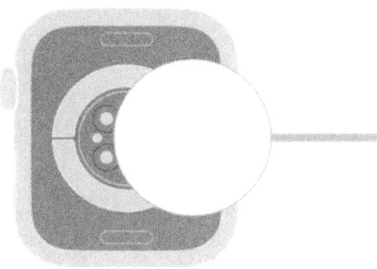

Watch Magnetic Quick Charger to USB-C, Concave Magnetically attaches to Watch's rear plate.

See Whether There Is Any Juice Left

Control Center may be accessed by touching and holding the bottom of the screen, then swiping up to see the battery percentage. Installing a battery complication on the watch face is a simple way to see how much juice is left.

The face of a watch with a % battery life complication.

Power down

Turning on Low Power Mode will extend the battery life. Doing this action disables the Always-On Display, as well as any background blood oxygen or heart rate monitoring and alerts. The delivery of emergency warnings may be delayed or even fail, and the availability of certain cellular and Wi-Fi networks may be restricted. The cellular connection is disabled unless it is needed, such as when playing a streaming music service or sending a text message.

As soon as the battery reaches 90% capacity, Low Power Mode will be disabled automatically.

Partial battery charge is shown by a yellow ring on the Low Power Mode screen, which also includes the words "39 percent battery left" and a Low Power Mode button.

1. To access the Control Center, press and hold the bottom of the screen.
2. Choose Low Power Mode by tapping the battery icon.
3. Once you're happy with your selection, hit the button labeled "Switch On Low Power Mode" to activate it.

You may choose 1 Day, 2 Days, or 3 Days by tapping Turn On For.

The remaining charge of any battery-powered items, like AirPods, that are Bluetooth-connected to your Watch will show up here.

Your Watch will notify you and provide you the option to switch to Low Power Mode when the battery level reaches 10 percent.

Go back to regular power operation.

1. To access the Control Center, press and hold the bottom of the screen.
2. To disable Low Power Mode, just tap the battery percentage.

Time Since the Last Charge Should Be Verified

There is 94% battery life according to Watch. Battery life is shown via a bar chart.

1. Launch the Watch's Settings menu.
2. Battery Tapping.

On the Battery screen, you can see how much battery life is left, when the battery was last charged, and a graph detailing the battery's recent charging history.

Battery health should be checked.

Your Watch's battery life may be measured in comparison to its capacity when it was first purchased.

1. Launch the Watch's Settings menu.
2. Choose Battery, and then Battery Health.

Your Watch will send you a notification when the battery life is becoming dangerously low, giving you time to consider your replacement alternatives.

Don't let applications auto-reload in the background.

When you transition to a new app, the previous app doesn't stay open or use any more resources; but, it may continue "refresh," or look for updates and new material.

Background app refreshes might be a power drain. If you want longer battery life, you may disable this feature.

1. Launch the Watch's Settings menu.
2. Choose Preferences > Automatic App Refresh.
3. To stop all applications from refreshing in the background, you may turn off Background App Refresh. Instead, you may disable refresh for certain applications by scrolling down.

The background app refresh option must be active for the current watch face's complications to update.

Activate & Deactivate Your Watch
Watch, please activate, and wake.

- Press and hold the side button until the Apple logo shows if the Watch is off (may see a dark screen).
- Watch faces display on active watches.
- To turn off your Watch, press and hold the side button until the sliders show, then push the Power button in the upper right.
- Pressing and holding the Digital Crown when the Watch is off displays the time.

Watch the display with the Power Off button highlighted. With a quick swipe of the slider, you can disable Watch.

Your Watch cannot be turned off while charging. After you're done using your Watch, remove it from its charging dock.

Always On

The Always On option may be found in the Display & Brightness settings menu.

If you have a Watch that supports it, putting your wrist down won't prevent the watch face from showing the current time thanks to Always On. The watch's full functionality is activated when the wrist is raised.

Always On is disabled in Low Power Mode on your Watch. Tap the screen to see the watch's face.

Always On is compatible with the Watch Series 5, Series 6, Series 7, and Series 9 models.

1. Launch the Watch's Settings menu.
2. To keep the screen on permanently, choose the Always On option under Display & Brightness.
3. To customize the following features, activate Always On and then press the corresponding toggles:
    o Select the complications that have information shown when the wrist is lowered.
    o Choose which alerts will be shown when you put down your wrist.
    o Display Apps lets you choose which programs will be shown when the user places their hand below their wrist.

Initiate the Watch screen.

The Watch display may be woken up in the following ways by default:

- Extend your wrist upward. When you put your arm down, your Watch goes back to sleep.
- Choose options with a tap of the screen or the turn of the Digital Crown.
- Adjust the Digital Crown by raising it.

Open Watch Settings and choose Display & Brightness. You may deactivate Wake on Wrist Raising and Wake on Crown Rotation to prevent the watch from awakening when you elevate your wrist or rotate the Digital Crown.

Theater mode prevents your Watch from waking up when you raise your wrist.

If Watch does not wake when you lift your wrist, alter its orientation. Your Watch may be dead and require charging if touching the screen or rotating the Digital Crown does not activate it.

To the clock face

The watch lets you set the time it takes for the watch to go back to the clock face after navigating away from an app.

1. Launch the Watch's Settings menu.
2. To set a certain time for your Watch to revert to the clock face, choose General > Return to Clock

and then scroll down to the appropriate time. In any case, after two minutes or at the latest hour.
3. Moreover, you may use the Digital Crown to get back to the time display.

A single setting affects all applications, but you may also specify individual times for each one if you choose. Choose an app from the list, then touch Custom, and finally select a preference.

Awaken To Your Last Task

In certain cases, you may have Watch wake up just where you left off in an app. Audiobooks, maps, mindfulness, music, now playing, podcasts, stopwatches, timers, voice memos, walkie-talkies, and workouts are just some of the applications available.

1. Launch the Watch's Settings menu.
2. Choose an app from the drop-down menu, then activate Return to App by going to Settings > General > Return to Clock.

Stopping whatever you were doing in the app (a podcast, a Maps route, a timer) will bring you back to the clock face.

You may also access this feature by launching the Watch app on your iPhone and selecting My Watch > General > Return to Clock.

You may prolong the life of your Watch screen by keeping it on for longer.

When you touch the Watch to wake it up, you may leave the screen on for a longer period.

1. Launch the Watch's Settings menu.
2. Choose Wake for 70 Seconds by going to Display & Brightness > Wake Duration.

Secure Or Unlock The Watch

Open Watch

You may unlock your Watch with a passcode or by just unlocking your iPhone.

- Type in the security code: The watch requires a wake-up and password.
- A watch is unlocked when the iPhone is unlocked. To enable Unlock with iPhone, launch the Watch app on your iPhone, then choose My Watch > Passcode.

Your iPhone must be within Bluetooth range (10 meters, 33 feet) to activate Watch Touch ID. The watch needs a password if Bluetooth is off.

You need not use the same passcode for both your iPhone and Watch.

Set A New Passcode

There are three options for adjusting your Watch passcode: Turn the Passcode Off, Change the Passcode, and Unlock it with your iPhone.

You may modify the Watch passcode you put up first by doing the following:

1. Launch the Watch's Settings menu.
2. Follow the on-screen instructions after selecting Passcode, then afterward selecting Change Passcode.

You can also access this feature by launching the Watch app on your iPhone, selecting My Watch, tapping Passcode, and finally selecting Change Passcode.

If you want to use a passcode that is more than four digits long, you may disable Simple Passcode in the Settings app on your Watch.

Disable the security code.

1. Launch the Watch's Settings menu.
2. Choose the Passcode option, and then select the Off button.

To disable the passcode on your Watch, launch the Watch app on your iPhone and go to My Watch > Passcode > Toggle Passcode Off.

Apple Pay cannot be used if the password protection on your Watch is turned off.

Immediately Secure Lock

When you take off your Watch, it will automatically lock itself. Follow these steps to modify how your wrist is detected.

1. Launch the Watch's Settings menu.
2. To activate or deactivate Wrist Detection, tap Passcode.

If you disable wrist detection on your Watch, you won't be able to use the:

- If you want to make a purchase with Apple Pay on your Watch, you'll need to enter your passcode when you double-click the side button.
- There are gaps in our understanding of the Activity's true extent.
- We've disabled the heart rate monitor and all related alerts.
- The Watch will no longer lock and unlock mechanically.
- Even if the Watch detects a hard-impact fall, it will not immediately dial 911.

Use the Lock button in the Control Center's lower-right corner to manually lock the interface.

1. To access the Control Center, press and hold the bottom of the screen.
2. Click the Lock icon.

If you want to lock your Watch without using the wrist detection feature, you'll need to disable that feature. To disable wrist detection, go to your Watch's Settings > Passcode > Turn Passcode Off.

The next time you attempt to use your Watch, you'll be prompted to enter a passcode.

You may prevent inadvertent touches while working out by locking your screen. If you want to lock your Watch while using the Workout app, just swipe right. Water Lock prevents accidental unlocking of your Watch when swimming.

If you lose your secret code

Password-protecting your Watch requires erasing the device if you ever lose access. Here are several strategies to accomplish that goal:

- If you want to reset your Watch and forget the passcode, you'll need to unpair it from your iPhone and then pair it again.
- You may try reconnecting your Watch to your iPhone once you've reset it.

After ten failed tries to unlock the Watch, it will be erased.

If your Watch is ever lost or stolen, you may secure your data by setting it to delete all of its contents after 10 failed tries to open it with the erroneous password.

1. Launch the Watch's Settings menu.
2. Choose the Wipe Data passcode and tap the switch.

The watch's language and orientation may be changed.

Switch To Other Language / Country

As long as you have your iPhone set up to recognize several languages, your Watch will be able to show material in any of those languages.

1. Get out your iPhone and launch the Watch app.
2. You may choose a language by selecting My Watch, then General, then Language & Region, and finally Custom.

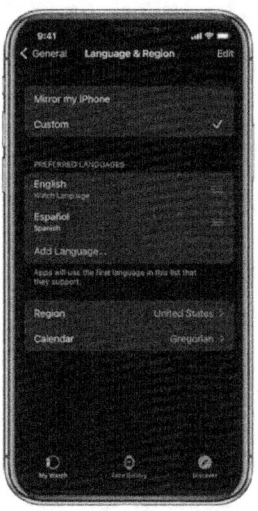

Watch the app's Language & Region screen, with English and Spanish listed as Preferred Languages.

Flip Your Wrists Digital Crown

Adjust your Watch's orientation if you wish to wear it on the other wrist or if you want the Digital Crown on the other side, and then arrange it such that waking it up involves lifting your wrist and spinning the crown in the desired way.

1. Launch the Watch's Settings menu.
2. Choose Settings and then Orientation.

On the iPhone, you can access this setting by opening the Watch app, selecting My Watch, and then selecting General > Watch Orientation.

On Watch, you'll find the Orientation menu. The Digital Crown and the wrist may be customized.

Watch Bands Are Easily Removed, Swapped Out, And Refastened

Remove, replace, and secure your bands following these guidelines.

Always match band size to watch case. The Watch Series 4, 5, SE, 6, 7, SE (2nd Generation), and 9 are compatible with bands from the original Watch or the first three generations. The bands for 39mm, 40mm, 41mm, 42mm, 44mm, and 45mm cases are interchangeable.

Every Watch up to Series 9 may utilize bands from Series 4, 5, 6, 7, SE (2nd Gen), and Series 9. Solo Loop or Braided Solo Loop bands work with Watch Series 4, 5, SE, 6, 7, SE (2nd Generation), and 9. Watch Series 4, 5, SE, 6, 7, SE (2nd Generation), and 9 accept bands from older models.

Bands may be taken off and switched.

1. Press the band release button. Hold down the Watch band release button.
2. Slide the band to one side to unfasten and insert the new band.

    Never jam a band into the opening. If you have trouble removing or inserting a band, push the band release button again.

A Different shot of a Watch. With the illustration on the left, you may quickly and easily release the band. The watch band on the right may be seen halfway fitted into the band hole.

Band it together

The Watch functions best when it is snug on the wrist.

To use the Watch's wrist recognition, haptic alerts, and heart rate sensor, the back of the device must be in direct touch with your skin. Comfort and accurate sensor readings come from wearing your Watch in just the right way, which means not too tight, not too loose, and with enough breathing space for your skin. Moreover, the sensors are only activated when the Watch is worn on the top of the wrist.

CHAPTER TWO

HOW TO SET UP A RELATIVE'S WATCH

You may control the Watch for a parent or schoolchild without an iPhone. Family Sharing modifications need a parent/guardian or group organizer.

To see settings and download software updates, the iPhone you used to connect and set up the Watch must be within Bluetooth range (33 feet or 10 meters). Someone in your Family Sharing group must have a Watch SE or Watch Series 4 with cellular capabilities to set up a Watch. The iPhone that controls the watch may utilize a separate cellular service.

Family formation isn't possible anywhere.

Screen Time on the iPhone allows several adjustments with the Watch app:

- Barriers to communication and the need for secure networks
- Set aside regular breaks from your screen time.

- School time is a Watch feature that disables or restricts access to certain apps and functions while in school.
- Options for configuring email and scheduling in iCloud, Google, and other cloud storage services
- Settings to limit access to sexually explicit material, in-app purchases, and personal information

You can also view the managed Watch's Activity, Health, and Location info, depending on setup.

Family members can't set up a Watch to connect with the iPhone. You can't transfer duties from the controlled Watch to the iPhone or unlock a family member's iPhone from your Watch. An iPhone app used to set up a family member's Watch cannot be deleted.

Set Up Watch For A Relative

Getting a loved one set up with a Watch is as simple as setting up your own. Erase the watch to make sure it is completely blank before pairing and setting it up for a family member.

1. Instruct the family members to don their Watches. It's possible to customize the Watch's band size to ensure a snug yet comfortable fit on the wearer's wrist.

2. Just press and hold the side button until the Apple logo shows to activate the Watch.
3. With your iPhone within range of the Watch, wait for the iPhone to display the Watch pairing screen, and then touch Proceed.

Instead, you might launch the Watch app on your iPhone; go to My Watch, then All Watches, and finally Add Watch.

Apple's Watch application icon

4. Choose Family Member Setup, and then click Proceed.
5. Arrange your iPhone so that the Watch is visible in the Watch app's viewfinder when requested to do so. It's a matching set for the two gadgets.
6. Choose the Watch setup option. To complete the setup, just stick to the on-screen prompts on your iPhone and watch.

Oversee The Watch Of A Family Member
1. Launch the Watch application on the iPhone.
2. After selecting "My Watch," "Family Watches," and a specific timepiece, "Done" will appear.

The following options are shown when you choose My Watch for a monitored watch:

Setting	Options
General	Check for updates, change language and region, and reset Apple Watch.
Cellular	Set up cellular if you haven't.
Accessibility	Configure accessibility settings.
Emergency SOS	Turn on or off the option to hold the side button to call emergency services, and add and change emergency contacts.
School time	Set up a school time schedule.
Screen Time	Manage parental controls, get insights about your family member's screen time, and set limits.
Activity	Manage a fitness experience made for younger users.
Contacts	Choose trusted contacts.
Find My	Choose notification settings.
Handwashing	Manage restrictions, and turn the handwashing timer on or off.
Health	Add or edit health details and Medical ID, view the health data (with the proper permissions and settings) of the person who uses the managed Apple Watch, request to share health data, and choose to stop receiving health data.

Heart	View the heart data (with the proper permissions and settings) of the person who uses the managed Apple Watch, including heart rate, heart rate variability, resting heart rate, and walking heart rate average.
Mail & Calendar	Add a family member's account—Gmail or Outlook, for example. Also choose how often Apple Watch fetches calendar updates.
Messages	Choose dictation options, and edit smart replies.
Noise	Turn Environmental Sound Measurements on or off, and set the noise threshold.
Photos	Select a photo album from the iPhone used to manage the watch, and choose the number of photos Apple Watch can display.
Wallet & Apple Pay	Set up Apple Cash and Express Transit cards.

Timing Your Screen Use

Set up parental controls on a Watch using Screen Time. With Screen Time, you may restrict your child's access to certain websites and applications, as well as set time limits on their screen usage. You may also set restrictions on in-app purchases, the viewing of sexual material, and the sharing of location data.

These are the actions you need to take to activate Screen Time:

1. Launch the Watch application on the iPhone.

2. After selecting "My Watch," "Family Watches," and a specific timepiece, "Done" will appear.
3. To activate Screen Time, choose it from the menu, then hit the Settings cog.
4. In the following windows, you may set parameters for blocked material, secure communication, screen time, and app/website use limitations.
5. Make a password for Screen Time.

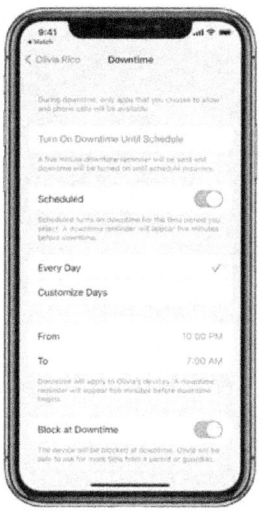

A Device configuration screen for Downtime on an iPhone. Somewhere towards the top is a timed switch. Below it, you'll have the choice to either use Every Day or Configure Days. The hours of operation, both from and to, are located in the

screen's central portion, and a Block at Downtime button may be found at the screen's bottom.

A second option is to access the Screen Time settings by opening the Settings app on the iPhone, tapping Screen Time, tapping the name of the family member under the Family heading, tapping Turn On Screen Time, and then configuring the Screen Time settings.

Use The School Time Watch App

Displays the date and digital time in the middle of the Schooltime analog clock face. The watch has a spot at the bottom for the user's name.

During the school day, the Watch's functionality is restricted by the "Schooltime" app so that parents and other caregivers may concentrate on their children.

Schedule Classes

1. Launch the Watch application on the iPhone.

2. Choose My Watch, then Family Watches, and finally a timepiece.
3. Finish by selecting the Schooltime option.
4. Enable Schooltime and then choose the Modify Schedule option.
5. Choose the times of day and days of the week when Schooltime will be active on your watch.
6. If you wish to create various schedules for different times of day, such as 9:00 a.m. to 12:00 p.m. and 1:00 p.m. to 3:00 p.m., tap Add Time.

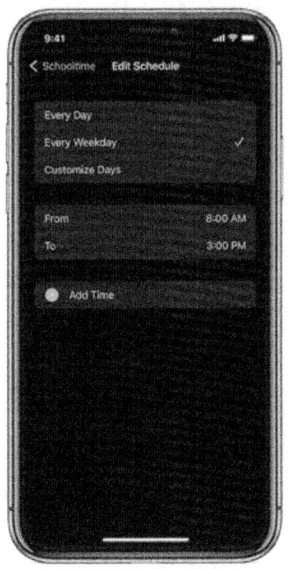

Example of the Schooltime schedule editing interface on an iPhone. Optional drop-down menus for "Every Day," "Every Weekday," and "Customize Days" are shown, with "Every Weekday" chosen.

Time may be added between and to points in the screen's center.

Get Out of School Free Card

Take a break from Schooltime so that your child may check their activity rings, for instance.

Choose "Exit" by tapping the screen, then pressing and holding the Digital Crown.

If you leave Schooltime within the designated hours, the Schooltime watch face will automatically reappear when you lower your wrist. Until the next planned start time or until you hit the Schooltime button in the Control Center, Schooltime does not function outside of its regular hours.

Find Out The Exact Moment When Class Time Was Made Available

You will get a report that details the time and duration of your family member's leave from Schooltime. Here's what you need to do to access the report:

1. Launch the Watch application on the iPhone.
2. Choose My Watch, then Family Watches, and finally a timepiece.

3. After tapping "Done," choose "Schooltime" to get reports detailing when and for how long Schooltime was activated.

A Watch version of the report is also available. Schooltime may be seen by opening the Watch's Settings app and tapping the appropriate section.

If you put the screen to sleep, school time will resume.

If your child has joined a study group outside school hours and needs to concentrate, they may switch on Schooltime at any time. Just press your finger down on the bottom of the screen, drag it up to reveal Control Center, and then hit the Schooltime icon. On the Game Boy Advance, press and hold the Digital Crown until the Schooltime menu appears, and then choose Exit. When it is time, or when you manually activate it in the Control Center, the school will start up again.

Get Health And Activity Reports

Together with your loved one, set daily exercise goals and monitor improvement to have a clearer picture of their level of activity. Medical records are available to you with the patient's permission.

Include a loved one in your daily routine by setting activity objectives for them.

Children who use a Watch under parental supervision may set activity objectives in terms of move minutes rather than active calories. Minutes of vigorous action (running, leaping, and playing) is the target for exercise, and outdoor run, walk, and bike exercises are designed specifically for kids under the age of 13.

If you're the one managing a family member's Watch, you can choose between a younger and an older fitness experience, independent of the user's real age.

1. Launch the Watch app on the iPhone serving as the controller.
2. Choose My Watch, then Family Watches, and finally a timepiece.
3. Just hit "Done," "Activity," and then toggle "Less than 13 years old" off or on.

If the family member has a Watch, they can do this from their wrist by going to the Watch's Settings menu, tapping Activities, and toggling the "Under 13 years old" setting.

Check out the latest progress report

1. Open the Health app on your iPhone once you've established physical activity targets for a family member.
2. Choose the Sharing tab, and then select the appropriate family member's name under the Sharing with you heading.
3. Click the "Activities" tab.
4. You may observe your loved one's daily activities up to that point by tapping the timeline.

Data may be seen on an annual, monthly, weekly, or daily basis.

Refer to the health resources.

If your loved one has permitted you, you may monitor their hearing health and heart rate in addition to their activities.

1. Access the Sharing option inside Health on your iPhone.
2. Choose the loved one's name from the Sharing with You list.
3. Choose a health category by tapping the corresponding button.

Provide medical information and a photo ID

In case you forgot to include a loved one's medical information during setup, you may do it now by following these measures:

1. Launch the Watch application on the iPhone.
2. Choose My Watch, then Family Watches, and finally a timepiece.
3. Choose an action from the list below after tapping done and selecting Health.
   - Choose "Health Information" to add or modify demographic data such as your birthday, height, and weight.
   - To edit your medical ID and add important information like emergency contacts, choose the corresponding menu option.

Both the iPhone used to run the Watch and the watch itself display health information and Medical ID.

- Here is what it looks like on your iPhone: To see a family member's profile, launch the Health app, go to Sharing, press the name of the member of the family, and finally, choose Profile.
- The Health app may be accessed by launching the Settings app on the controlled Watch and then tapping the Health tab.

Spend Apple Cash With Family

If you're the group administrator for Family Sharing, you may enable Apple Pay allowing your group's younger members to use their Watches to make in-app purchases and give and receive money using Messages. In addition, you may restrict your child's ability to transfer money to certain people, get alerts whenever the account is used, and even freeze the account if necessary.

Apple Cash requires an iPhone SE or later model iPhone to function and is not accessible in all locations.

Create a Family Pool with Apple Pay

The family members you're setting up Apple Cash for must be under the age of eighteen, and you must be the organizer of the family to do so.

1. Choose "Family Sharing" from the list of options under "Settings" > "[your name]" on your iPhone.
2. Choose a kid or adolescent and then tap Apple Pay.
3. To create an Apple Cash account, the user should choose the appropriate option and then follow the on-screen prompts.

Your American loved one may use Apple Pay to shop, transfer money, and receive money in the United States.

Family Members May Manage Apple Pay
1. Launch Wallet on the iPhone serving as the watch's controller.
2. Click the More buttons after tapping your Apple Cash card.
3. Choose a member of the family by tapping their name.
4. Prepare the following choices:
   - You get to decide who in the family may get the money.
   - You may choose to get alerts whenever a close relative makes a purchase.
5. By selecting the Send Money button, you may access Apple Pay from the Messages app.

To prohibit a family member from using Apple Pay or transferring money over Messages, choose Lock Apple Cash.

Both open the Wallet app on your iPhone and touch your Apple Cash card to view a family member's purchases or use the Transactions tab on this screen. Under Recent Transactions and

Transactions in [year], you'll see your loved ones' purchases and payments.

CHAPTER THREE

HOW TO USE WATCH APPLICATIONS

From the Watch's main menu, you may access any of the available apps. The Dock allows you to quickly access your most used programs. The Dock allows you to permanently save up to 10 of your most frequently used applications.

Project your applications in a grid or a list format

The Home Screen supports both a grid and a list layout for its app presentation. How to pick:

1. You may access the Home Screen by touching and holding it.
2. Choose either a grid or a list to see the data.

Grid View and List View tabs may be seen on the View Settings page. At the very bottom of your screen is the option to Edit Applications.

Launch Software By Touching
Launch Software By Touching Its Icon On The Desktop

Whatever perspective you choose is how the app will be launched.

- For a grid view, choose the app's icon. If you're currently on the Home Screen and want to launch the app in the middle of the screen, just spin the Digital Crown.

Watch's home screen displays in grid format, grouping applications. You may launch a program by tapping its icon. You may expand the list of available applications by dragging the slider.

- Examining a list: Choose an application with a turn of the Digital Crown.

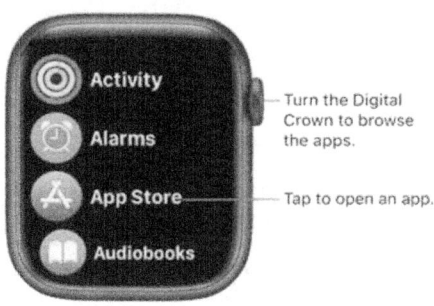

The Watch's home screen displays the applications in a list. Launch a program with a tap. Keep scrolling to see other options.

Just touch the Digital Crown once to exit an app return to the Home Screen, and press it again to choose between watch faces (or, in grid view, tap the watch icon on the Home Screen).

If you double-click the Digital Crown while viewing an app or the watch face, it will launch the last app you were using.

Start A Program From The Dock
1. You may move between the Dock's applications by pressing the side button and then turning the Digital Crown.
2. Launch a program with a tap.

The Calendar app in the Dock, with the All Applications button below. To access other software, you may turn on the Digital Crown. Just tapping on it will unlock it.

Alter Programs Shown In The Dock

The Dock may display your most frequently used applications or up to 10 of your absolute favorites.

- Access a list of recently used programs here. Open the Dock app on your Watch and choose Recents to retrieve recent settings. The Dock shows the presently active application at the top and the most recently used programs in reverse chronological order.
- Select My Watch from the Dock menu on the iPhone to view Watch Recents.
- Identify your most-used programs: Choose Dock from iPhone Watch. Add additional apps to your favorites by going to Favorites, Edit, and Plus.

Click and drag the Reorder button to reorder. When finished, press done.

- Press the side button and use the Digital Crown to choose an app to remove from the Dock. Close the app with a left swipe and X.

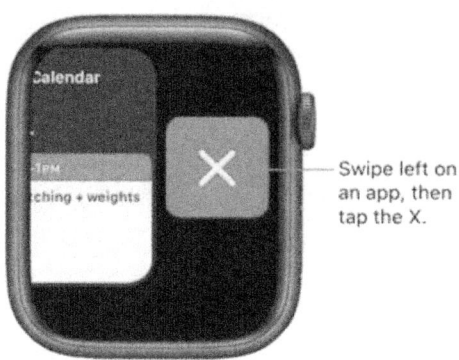

Swipe left on an app, then tap the X.

When you swipe left on an app, the Dock will appear, and the X button will be on the right.

- To access the Home Screen instead of the Dock, press and hold the Dock button. Underneath the Dock, choose All Applications.

Whether you have your app list set to show Recents or Favorites, the applications that have active sessions (such as a Map will always be shown at the top of the list.

Watch App Management

Place Your Programs In A Grid Format

1. To enter the Watch's Home Screen, press the Digital Crown.
   Touch and hold the Home Screen to switch between list and grid views. Instead, use Watch Settings to obtain Grid View.
2. Tap and hold an app, then choose Edit Apps.
3. Reposition the app by dragging.
4. To terminate, tap the Digital Crown.

Touch and hold an app, then drag to a new location.

The grid layout of the Watch's Home screen.

The iPhone Watch app's My Watch > App View > Arrange option is another alternative. Touch and hold an icon to slide it to reorder app icons.

When seen in a list, applications are always sorted alphabetically.

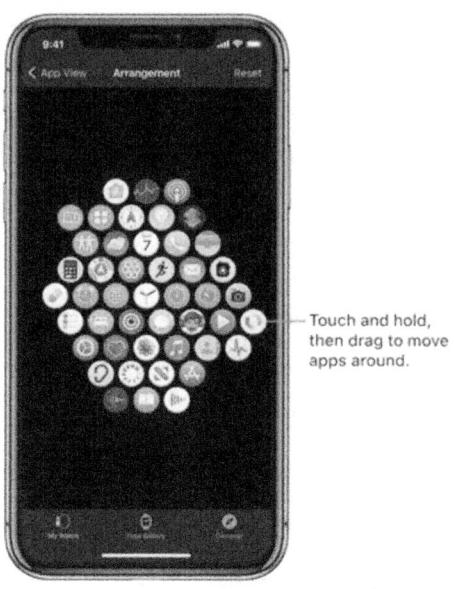

An indicator grid on the Watch app's Arrangement screen.

Remove an app from Watch

To delete an app from your Watch, touch and hold the Home screen, choose Edit Applications, and then select the X. unless you also remove it from the linked iPhone, it will stay on that device.

You can also delete an app from your Watch by swiping left on it in the list view and then tapping the Trash icon.

You cannot uninstall all applications from your Watch.

Modify your app's preferences

1. Get out your iPhone and launch the Watch app.
2. To see the applications you've added to your watch, choose My Watch and scroll down.
3. Modify an app's preferences with a tap.

The Watch is similarly subject to the limitations you set on your iPhone under Settings > Screen Time > Content & Privacy Restrictions. If you turn off the Camera on your iPhone, the Watch will no longer display the Camera Remote app.

Verify how much space is being used by applications.

You may see the overall storage utilized the available storage, and the storage used by each program on your Watch.

1. Launch the Watch's Settings menu.
2. Follow the prompts to the Storage section in the General settings.

To use this feature on your iPhone, launch the Watch app, choose My Watch, and then go to General > Storage.

Watch Allows You To Check The Time
The Watch has many methods of displaying time.

- You may check the time by raising your wrist; most applications and the watch face itself display the time, as does the grid view clock.
- Take note of the hour: Just activate Speak Time by going to the Watch's Settings > Clock > Speaking. To listen to the time, place two fingers on the display.

  On the hour, the Watch can also play a chime. Turn on Chimes by selecting Clock in the Settings app on your Watch. You may choose between bells or birds by tapping the Sounds button.

- Feel the time: Open the Settings app on your Watch, choose Clock, select Taptic Time, switch on Taptic Time, and then select an option to have the time tapped out on your wrist while the Watch is in quiet mode.

A watch may be programmed to always announce the time if Taptic Time is turned off. Taptic Time requires Control With Quiet Mode to be enabled in Settings > Clock > Speak Time.

- You may ask Siri the time by raising your wrist and saying "What time is it?"

Make Use Of Watch App, "Focus"

Focusing your attention and clearing your mind will allow you to take pleasure in the activity at hand. Focus tells other users and programs that you're currently occupied and filters incoming notifications to just those that are relevant to your current task.

You may choose from three different focus modes—"Personal," "Sleep," and "Work." In addition to setting up which apps are allowed to send you notifications and when you can modify your iPhone's Focus to suit your needs.

To make your iPhone's Focus settings accessible on all of your other devices that use the same Apple ID, go to Settings > Focus and then select the Share across Devices button.

Focus On/Off Toggle

Do Not Disturb, Personal, Work, and Sleep are shown as options in the Focus menu.

1. To access the Control Center, press and hold the bottom of the screen.
2. Tap and hold the current Focus button then press a new Focus.

   While Focus is not active, the Do Not Disturb option appears in the Control Center.

3. Choose a Focus time frame, such as On, On for 1 hour, Today, Tomorrow, or Until I Leave.

Turning off a Focus is as easy as tapping its button in the Control Center.

Each Focus has its symbol that shows in various places on the watch face, in applications next to the time, and Control Center when it is active.

Make up your Mindset

1. To change the iPhone's focus settings, tap the Settings > Focus menu.
2. You'll need to follow the on-screen prompts after tapping the Add button to add a Focus.

   While making a personalized concentration, you may give it a color, an icon, and a name.

Choose a watch dial from Focus

Assigning a unique watch face to each Focus allows you to easily distinguish between them. Your Watch may, for instance, switch to the Simple watch face while the Work Focus mode is on.

1. Access this feature by tapping the Focus option in the iPhone's Settings menu.
2. Choose a Focus from the list, or add a new one by tapping Set Up next to it, followed by Customize Focus and Pick (located just below the Watch icon).
3. Tap the Done button after choosing a watch face.

Prepare Yourself To Focus

You may schedule your Focuses on Watch to start at certain times of the day if you choose. Focused work time, for instance, may begin at 9:00 AM PST and last until midnight MST, Monday through Friday. Concentration lapses or a new sort of Focus may take over between noon and 1:00 p.m. Get back to it between 1 and 5 p.m. throughout the week.

1. Launch the Watch's Settings menu.
2. Choose "Focus," then "Add new" and a specific focus, such as "Work."
3. To choose when the Focus should start and stop, tap the corresponding from and to fields.
4. Just scroll down and choose the days you'd want the Focus to be on.

5. Focus may be saved by tapping in the upper left corner.
6. To include other actions in the Focus, just repeat the steps above.

The Monday through Friday, 9 a.m. to 5 p.m. schedule is shown on the Work Focus screen. There's a new entry button down here.

Turn off or remove a Focus appointment

If you no longer need a Focus schedule, you may either deactivate it or remove it by doing one of the following:

- To turn off a Focus, go to the Watch's settings, choose Focus, and then select the Focus you want to turn off. To disable a schedule, select it, scroll to the bottom, and tap the Enabled toggle.
  When you're ready to use the schedule again, just click the Enabled button.

- To remove a Focus from your Watch's schedule, open the Settings app, go to Focus, and then choose a Focus to remove it. Choose a timetable by tapping it, scrolling to the bottom, and then tapping Erase.

Alter the Watch's Visuals & Typeface

Alter the Watch's Visuals, Typeface, Sound, and Touch Feedback

Brightness may be adjusted using the slider at the top of the Display & Brightness options, and text size can be changed using the button at the bottom.

To modify the Watch's display and brightness, launch the Settings app and go to Display & Brightness.

- For Brightness, press the Brightness settings, or hit the slider and spin the Digital Crown.

- For larger or smaller text, choose Text Size and then use the Digital Crown to zoom in or out.
- Make this bold: Activate Bold Text.

The iPhone also allows for similar customizations. Adjust the brightness and font size in the Watch app by opening it on your iPhone, selecting My Watch, tapping Display & Brightness, and then selecting the appropriate options.

Alter Volume

1. Launch the Watch's Settings menu.
2. The Power of Touch and Music.
3. If you want to change the volume of an alert, press the slider under "Alert Volume" and then use the Digital Crown to make the necessary adjustments.

The Watch's Sounds & Haptics menu, including the Alert Volume slider and the Quiet Mode toggle.

You can also adjust the alert volume by launching the Watch app on your iPhone, selecting Sounds & Haptics, and then adjusting the slider next to Alert Volume.

The volume of headphones linked to your Watch may also be lowered. To disable excessive volume when using headphones, open the Settings app and go to Sounds & Haptics > Headphone Safety.

The Haptic Alerts Switch

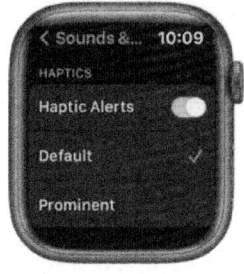

The Haptic Alerts switch, along with the Default and Prominent choices below it, can be found in the Watch's Sounds & Haptics settings.

The vibrations or taps on your wrist that the Watch uses to notify you may be customized.

1. Launch the Watch's Settings menu.
2. Haptic Alerts may be activated by going to Settings > Sounds & Haptics.
3. Make a Featured or Default selection.

Instead, you may access the Watch settings from the iPhone app by going to Watch > My Watch > Sounds & Haptics > Default or Prominent.

Toggle The Haptic Feedback

If you use the Watch's Digital Crown to scroll, you'll hear and feel clicks as you go. Here's how to disable or enable these haptics:

1. Launch the Watch's Settings menu.
2. Choose Sound & Haptics and toggle the status of Crown Haptics.

    The haptic feedback from the system may be toggled on or off as well.

If you prefer, you may disable or enable Crown Haptics from your iPhone by opening the Watch app, going to My Watch, and tapping Sounds & Haptics.

The Crown Haptics display, with the toggle, is enabled. Check out the System Haptics toggle below.

Tape In The Time

In quiet mode, the Watch will tap out the time on your wrist in a clear sequence.

1. Launch the Watch's Settings menu.
2. Choose Taptic Time by pressing Clock and then scrolling down.
3. Launch Taptic Time and choose your preferred display mode, from Digits, Terse, and Morse code.

- During the hours, the Watch double-taps every 10 hours, single-taps every hour afterward, double-taps every 10 minutes thereafter, and single-taps every minute thereafter.
- Sparse: every five hours, your Watch will make a long tap, then every hour and a half will make a short tap, and finally every quarter of an hour will make a long tap.
- Watch displays the time in Morse code by tapping out each number.

Taptic Time on the iPhone may also be customized. To activate Taptic Time, launch the Watch app on your iPhone, choose My Watch, then Clock > Taptic Time.

A watch may be programmed to always announce the time if Taptic Time is turned off. Taptic Time requires Control with Quiet Mode to be enabled in Settings > Clock > Speak Time.

CHAPTER FOUR

HOW TO CHECK YOUR WATCH FOR ALERTS

You may check and respond to meeting invitations, messages, noise alerts, and Activity reminders all from the convenience of your wrist with the help of your Watch. Your Watch may display notifications in real-time, but they will be queued up until you have a chance to look at them.

Reply A Message Sent To You

1. Raise your wrist if you hear or feel a notification, and look at its contents.

   The notification's appearance shifts from active to idle mode.

   - An active display has a little banner at the screen's top.
   - While the screen is unattended, a full-screen alert will show up.
2. You may read the alert by tapping on it.
3. If you want to dismiss a notification, just swipe down on it. You may also swipe up from the bottom of the alert to dismiss it.

The Watch alert for Noise. In the upper left corner, you should see the app's symbol that is linked to the alert. Just tapping it will launch the app.

See Your Unread Messages

Notifications that are ignored are stored in the Notification Center until you can deal with them. When you have unread notifications, your watch will display a red dot in the upper-right corner of the screen. Here's what you have to do to see it:

1. You may access the Notification Center from the watch face by swiping down. If you're on a different screen, touch and hold the top, then swipe down.

   When viewing the Watch Home Screen, you will not have access to the Notification Center. Notification Center may be accessed by pressing the Digital Crown after you've navigated to a watch face or app.

2. To see the whole list of alerts, swipe up or down, or use the Digital Crown to navigate left and right.
3. You may read or reply to the alert by tapping on it.

With a quick swipe to the left and the X, you may dismiss a notice from the Notification Center without ever opening it. To dismiss all alerts at once, swipe up to the menu bar and choose Clear All.

To access a notice from a group, you must first open the group by tapping on it.

Go to the Watch's Settings menu, choose Notifications, and then off the Notifications Indicator to get rid of the red dot.

Swipe down to view unread notifications.

When you have an unread alert, a red dot will show in the exact middle of your watch face.

Turn off Watch alerts altogether

The Watch Touch's quiet mode is accessed by holding the bottom of the screen, swiping up to reveal the Control Center, and tapping the silent mode button.

A tap still indicates a new alert has arrived. If you want to avoid interruptions and noise, use these methods:

1. To access the Control Center, press and hold the bottom of the screen.
2. Choose "Focus" or "Do Not Disturb" from the menu.
3. Choose Do Not Disturb, then decide whether you want it On, On for 1 hour, on till tonight/tomorrow morning, or on until I depart.

An easy way to silence your Watch is to put your palm on the screen for three seconds whenever you get a notification. To verify if the mute is engaged, a little touch will be felt. Cover to Mute may be activated in the Watch's Settings by navigating to Sounds & Haptics and then to Cover to Mute.

Modify Watch Alert Settings

The Watch's app notifications will automatically sync with your iPhone if you haven't already done so. Yet, certain applications' notification interfaces are modifiable.

A family member's Watch that you're responsible for won't follow your mirrored preferences.

Choose Which Applications Notify You
1. Get out your iPhone and launch the Watch app.
2. Choose Notifications from the "My Watch" menu.
3. Choose the app (say, Messages), then hit Custom, and finally make a selection. Choices might involve:
   - If you choose to enable push notifications, the app will send alerts to the system's Notification Center.
   - When you send a notice to the Notification Center, your Watch will not vibrate or show the notification on its screen.
   - You will not get any alerts from the app if you turn off notifications.
4. Adjust how the app's alerts are categorized. Choices may be made from among the following:
   - Turned off: Individual alerts are not consolidated into larger groups.
   - Automatically: Information from apps may be used to organize your Watch's notifications. Notifications on breaking news, for instance, will be organized into distinct folders for CNN,

the Washington Post, and People, depending on which outlets you choose to follow.
- Notifications are categorized by the app they originated from.

You may customize the kind of alerts you get in certain applications. You may choose the types of invitations or modifications to shared calendars that trigger Calendar alerts. Choose which email addresses may issue alerts in Mail.

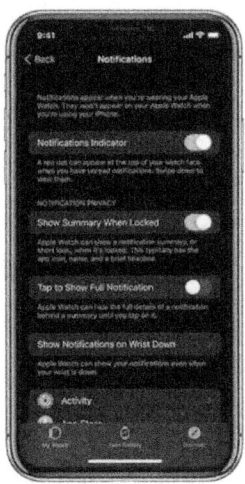

The iPhone app for the Watch has a Notification screen that lists the various alerts you may get.

A Medium To Modify Alert Settings
Choose Your Watch As The Medium To Modify Alert Settings

Swiping left on notice and selecting more brings up a menu where you may modify additional notification settings straight from your Watch. Choices might involve:

- Mute for 1 hour or Mute for Today: Notifications are sent straight to the Notification Center without the Watch producing a sound or showing the notice for the next hour or the rest of the day, respectively. Swipe left on a notice to see more menus, and then hit Unmute to restore the notification's visibility and sound.
- Further Information for the Synopsis: The Notification Summary is where you will see app-specific alerts in the future on your iPhone.

  You may restore instant notifications from the app by going to the iPhone's Settings menu, tapping Notifications, selecting the app in question, and finally selecting Immediate Delivery.

- Do not use a Focus that delays most alerts if you want to get time-sensitive notifications as soon as they are sent. But if you don't want this app to send you any alerts at all, including urgent ones, then you may disable it here.

- Disabling push notifications does not affect the app. Launch the Watch app on your iPhone, then go to My Watch > Notifications > the app you want to modify > Enable Notifications.

Configuring Watch notifications. There's a "Mute for 1 Hour" button-up top. Adding to the Summary, disabling Time Sensitive, and turning off are all options down below.

The lock screen should provide alerts.

When you lock your Watch, you have options for how alerts are shown.

1. Launch the Watch's Settings menu.
2. Go to the Notifications menu.
3. Choose a response from the following list.
    - If you enable the setting to "Show Summary While Locked," your Watch will provide a brief overview of unread notifications even when it is in its locked state. The summary has

a short headline, the app that alerts you to something, and the app's name and symbol.
- As you lift your wrist to check a notification, a summary will appear, followed by the complete information a few seconds later when you tap the notice. When a new message comes, for instance, you'll first see the sender's name, followed by the message itself. If you enable this setting, the entire notice will not show up until you touch it first.
- Turn on Wrist-Down Notifications: While your wrist is down, the Watch will not display alerts. If you enable this feature, your Watch will display alerts even when it is face down.

Adjust Your Apple Id Preferences

The details of your Apple ID are accessible for editing. You have the option of adding and updating your details, including contact information, a trusted phone number, and a password.

Adjust Your Address & Phone Number
1. Launch the Watch's Settings menu.
2. Choose [your login name].
3. Choose Contact Info after which you may choose from the following options:
    - Rename yourself: Choose your name from the menu and then select First, Middle, or Last.

- Look at, change, and add a contact: Choose an option for How to Contact Me and provide a phone number or email address. Choose the email address you want to delete, and then select the corresponding Delete Email Address button.
- Don't forget to provide contact information: If you want to add an email or phone number, choose that option from the menu that appears after tapping Add Email or Phone Number, press next, fill in the required fields, and then tap done.
- Cover your email address: Go On to the Next. You may choose to have applications contact you without them accessing your actual email address. If you choose this option, Apple will generate a random email address on your behalf; all messages received to this address from the app will be sent to your specified address.
- Substitute Your Birth Year To change your birthdate, choose Birthday and then the appropriate date.
- Get updates, suggestions, and the Apple News newsletter: Turn on Announcements, get suggestions for applications, music, TV, and

more, and subscribe to Apple News under Subscriptions.

Take charge of your Apple ID's security and password management

1. Launch the Watch's Settings menu.
2. Choose [your login name].
3. Choose Password & Security and proceed with one of the following actions:
   - Make a new passcode for your Apple ID: Choose Password Change and then comply with the on-screen prompts.
   - To modify the "Sign in with Apple" settings for a specific app or website: Choose an app by clicking on the option that reads Applications You Can Use with Your Apple ID. To disconnect your Apple ID from the app, choose to Stop Using Apple ID. (The next time you attempt to sign in using the app, you may be prompted to establish a new account.)
   - To make changes to an existing trusted phone number or add a new one, press the number you want to modify or add, confirm it when required, and then hit Delete Phone Number. If you have just one trusted number, you will be prompted to input a new one before deleting the existing one. Just choose the

option to "Add a Trusted Phone Number" to include another contact's number in your contact's trusted list.
- If you want to sign in from a different device or iCloud.com, you'll need a verification code. Just choose Obtain Verification Code.

Log in to your account and handle your memberships

1. Launch the Watch's Settings menu.
2. Choose [your login name].
3. Choose Subscriptions, and then select an individual subscription to see its details (such as price and duration).
4. To terminate your subscription, use the corresponding cancel button.

You'll need to cancel several subscriptions on your iPhone.

Access and control your gadgets

1. Launch the Watch's Settings menu.
2. Choose [your login name].
3. To learn more about a certain gadget, scroll down and touch it.
4. If you don't know the device's identity, choose Delete from Account.

Speed Up Your Watch Experience Using Shortcuts

Both the "When Do I Need to Leave" and "Set Good Night" shortcuts may be found in the Shortcuts app on the Watch.

You can do actions with a single touch using the Shortcuts app on your Watch. You can shorten the time it takes to do things like obtain directions, make a top 25 playlist, and more on your iPhone by creating custom shortcuts. You may use shortcuts by either opening the Shortcuts app or incorporating them into your watch face as complications.

A watch doesn't support all iPhone shortcuts.

Do a quick fix

1. Launch the Watch's Shortcuts app.
2. Choose a quick option.

Include a time-saving complexity

1. Tap the watch face, and then touch Edit.
2. To address an issue, swipe left to access it and then press it.
3. Choose a shortcut by scrolling down to the Shortcuts section.

Please improve Watch by adding more quick-access features.

1. Get out your iPhone's Shortcuts app.
2. Choose a shortcut's more buttons located in its upper right corner for further options.
3. After the shortcut page has loaded, tap the Info button and toggle Show on Watch to the on position.

CHAPTER FIVE

HOW TO SET UP HANDWASHING

Most international health authorities recommend at least 20 seconds of hand washing, and the Watch can detect when you've started and prompt you to finish. A smartwatch may also serve as a gentle reminder to wash your hands after a long day at the office.

To activate Handwashing

1. To activate Handwashing, go to the Watch's Settings menu.
2. Initiate the Handwashing Timer by selecting the Handwashing option.

An automatic 20-second timer will begin counting down on your Watch as soon as it recognizes that you've begun washing your hands. It's recommended that you don't stop washing in less than 20 seconds.

The clock decrements the time it takes to wash one's hands, starting at 4.

Make use of Handwashing Reminders

When arriving home, the Watch might prompt you to wash your hands.

1. Launch the Watch's Settings menu.
2. Choose "Handwashing," then "Handwashing Reminders," to activate the feature.

Reminders to wash your hands may also be set up on a Watch for a family member. To activate the Handwashing Timer and Reminders, go to Settings > General > Watch > Managed Watch > Handwashing.

Setting a home address in My Card inside the Contacts app on an iPhone is required to get handwashing reminders.

When you launch the Health app on your iPhone, choose Browse > Other Data > Handwashing to get a report detailing your typical handwashing sessions.

Join A Wireless Internet Connection

If you have your Watch connected to a Wi-Fi network, you can utilize many of its capabilities even if you don't have your iPhone with you.

Choose A Wireless Network

1. To access the Control Center, press and hold the bottom of the screen.
2. To connect to a network, touch and hold the Wi-Fi button until its name appears, and then choose it.
   The Watch only works with 902.11b/g/n 2.4GHz Wi-Fi networks.
3. One of the following should be done if a password is needed to access the network:
   - Enter the passcode using the Watch's on-screen keypad (not available in all languages, Watch Series 7 and Watch Series 9 only).
   - Scrawl the password on the screen using your finger. Choose both upper and lower case letters with the Digital Crown.
   - Choose a password by tapping the Password button and picking one at random.
   - If you want to input a password, you may use the iPhone's keyboard.
4. Choose the Join option.

Private IP addresses are preferable for the watch.

The Watch employs a media access control (MAC) address, a private network address, on every Wi-Fi network it connects to. You may discontinue using a private address for a network if it is unable to utilize one (for example, to give parental controls or to identify your Watch as permitted to join).

1. To access the Control Center, press and hold the bottom of the screen.
2. Just press and hold the Wi-Fi button, and after selecting a network, you may access its details by touching and holding its name.
3. Disable your address book.

Keep Private Address enabled on all supported networks for maximum privacy. If you want to prevent anyone from following your Watch as you switch between various Wi-Fi networks, using a private address is a good idea.

You may forget about building a network

1. To access the Control Center, press and hold the bottom of the screen.
2. To join a network, touch and hold the Wi-Fi button, and then press the network's name.
3. Choose to Forget This Network from the menu.

If the network needs a password and you rejoin at a later time, you will need to provide that password again.

Communicate With External Audio Devices

Listen to music or podcasts on your Watch using wireless headphones or speakers without needing your iPhone.

Tip: AirPods that have been synced with an iPhone are now ready for usage with your Watch; all you have to do is hit play.

Plug In Your Wireless Headphones

Listening to most music on a Watch requires Bluetooth headphones or speakers (Siri, phone calls, voicemail, and voice memos play through the speaker on the Watch). To activate the exploration mode on your headphones or speakers, just follow the on-screen prompts or the manual provided. To use a Bluetooth device, do the following when it is ready:

1. Bluetooth may be accessed in the Watch's Settings menu.
2. If a gadget pops up, tap it.

Audiobooks, Music, Currently Playing, and Podcasts all include an AirPlay button you may use to access Bluetooth settings from the play screen.

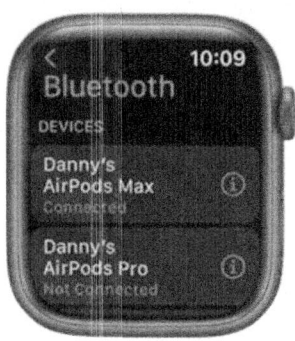 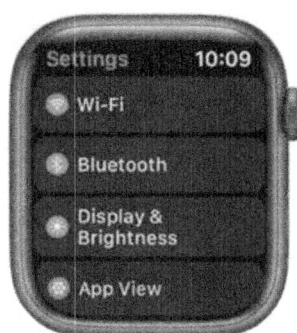

The display is split in half and placed side by side. The left-hand screen shows two Bluetooth devices, the linked AirPods Max and the unpaired AirPods Pro. On the right, you'll find the Settings menu, which includes tabs for Wi-Fi, Bluetooth, the screen's brightness and contrast, and the apps you last used.

You may choose an audio output.

1. To access the Control Center, press and hold the bottom of the screen.
2. Choose the desired audio output by tapping the corresponding icon.

Keep an eye on the acoustic levels of your headphones.

1. To access the Control Center, press and hold the bottom of the screen.
2. Tap the Headphone Volume button to adjust the volume when using headphones.

The volume of the headphones is shown on a meter.

Tone down the volume

The watch allows you to set a maximum volume for your headphones.

1. Launch the Watch's Settings menu.
2. Choose Headphone Safety from the Sounds & Haptics menu and then select Mute to lower the volume.
3. Adjust the volume by activating the feature to lower it.

Listen to alerts using headphones.

The watch will alert you with a headphone notice if you listen to your headphones at unsafely high volumes for an extended period, and it will reduce the volume for you automatically.

See the iPhone's notification history for your headphones by opening the Health app, tapping Browse, tapping Hearing, tapping Headphone

Notifications, and finally tapping a notice to see its information.

The Watch Is A Handy Tool For Passing Off Responsibilities

Handoff allows you to go from one device to another without interrupting your current task. You may respond to emails on your Watch using the Mail app, but you may want to use the iPhone's on-screen keyboard instead. You may use Handoff with a Watch that you've set up for yourself, but not with a family member's Watch.

1. Do something about your iPhone's lock.
2. To use the App Switcher on an iPhone equipped with Face ID, slide up from the bottom edge and pause. (Doubling-clicking the Home button on an iPhone will bring up the App Switcher.)
3. If you want to access the same content on your iPhone, tap the button that appears at the bottom of the screen.

If you don't see a button in App Switcher, check your iPhone's Settings > General > AirPlay & Handoff to make sure Handoff is enabled.

The handoff feature is enabled by default. The Watch app on the iPhone must be opened, the My

Watch tab selected, the General tab navigated to, and the Enable Handoff toggled off.

There are a wide variety of apps that are compatible with Handoff, including Activity, Alarm, Calendar, Home, Mail, Maps, Messages, Music, News, Phone, Podcasts, Reminders, Settings, Siri, Stocks, Stopwatch, Timers, Wallet, Weather, and World Clock. Connecting your Watch to your iPhone is required for the Handoff feature to function.

Transferring data from your Watch to a Mac is also possible if you're using OS X 10.10 or later.

Use Your Watch As A Password
Use Your Watch As A Password To Get Onto Your Computer

If you have a Watch and a Mac that was released after the middle of 2013, running macOS 10.13 or later, you can use it to quickly unlock your computer as soon as it comes up from sleep. Both your Computer and Watch must be signed in to iCloud with the same Apple ID.

If you want to know what year your Mac was manufactured, choose About This Mac from the Apple menu (found in the upper left corner of your screen). You can tell how old your Mac is by looking at its model name and seeing the year it was manufactured; for instance, "MacBook Pro (15-inch, 2019").

Switch On Auto-Unlock

1. Check that your gadgets are set up as follows:
   - Connectivity options like Wi-Fi and Bluetooth are active on your Mac.
   - Your Mac and Watch share the same Apple ID in iCloud, and you've enabled two-factor authentication for that Apple ID.
   - You've set up a passcode on your Watch.
2. Choose System Preferences from the Apple menu.
3. Choose General from the list that appears after selecting Security & Privacy.
4. Mark the box labeled "Use Watch to unlock applications and your Laptop."

If more than one Watch is in your possession, you may choose which ones will be used to access your Computer and applications.

If you haven't activated two-factor authentication for your Apple ID yet, please do so by following the on-screen instructions and then re-checking the box.

Release your Mac's security settings

With your wristwatch, you may easily wake your Mac without entering a password.

Joe's MacBook Pro was unlocked using this Watch, as shown on his wrist.

Have your Watch on your wrist, unlocked, and within proximity to your Laptop.

Use Watch To Unlock Your iPhone

Do the following to enable Watch to unlock your iPhone in response to a Siri request or when Face ID cannot be used due to an obstruction:

1. To activate Face ID and input your passcode on your iPhone, go to Settings > Face ID & Passcode.
2. Choose Unlock with Watch and activate your watch's security settings.
   Set all of your watches to "on" if you have more than one.

3. Wear your Watch, wake your iPhone, and then peek at its screen to unlock it.

If your iPhone is unlocked, the Watch will tap your wrist.

John's iPhone was unlocked using this Watch, as shown on his wrist. Thereafter, click the Lock iPhone button down below.

To use your Watch's passcode to unlock your iPhone, your Watch must be unlocked, on your wrist, and within range of your iPhone.

Put Watch To Use Without An iPhone
You can use your Watch even if your iPhone isn't nearby.

With an active cellular plan and a Watch that supports it, you can maintain contact with the outside world even when you're not near your iPhone. If you don't have an iPhone with you or access to Wi-Fi, you may still use your Watch.

- So, tune in!
- Listen to podcasts
- Listen to audiobooks
- Audio memos may be recorded and listened to afterward.
- Take use of student identification and public transportation cards
- Locate people, gadgets, and stuff
- A watch, world clock, alarm clock, stopwatch, and other timing devices
- See images from shared picture albums
- Use Apple Pay to pay for things at stores.
- Observe the scheduled activities
- Monitor your progress and exercise routine
- Relax and breathe deeply, monitor your pulse rate and blood oxygen levels, and keep note of your menstrual cycles.
- Check the ambient and in-ear noise levels.

While working out outside, the Watch's built-in GPS may provide more precise distance and speed data independent of an iPhone. The barometric altimeter in the Watch provides more precise data on elevation gain and loss. Even more precise is the always-on altimeter in Watch Series 6 and beyond, which displays your current elevation in real-time.

Your Watch can access the internet over Wi-Fi if it is set up properly.

Despite not having your iPhone nearby, you may still do the following tasks with your Watch when it is connected to Wi-Fi:

- Get the software from the App Store.
- Transmit Messages
- Talk on the phone (if Wi-Fi calling is turned on, or if you wish to use FaceTime's audio calling feature when near a Wi-Fi network).
- Use a Walkie-Talkie
- Play audio on your Watch using iTunes Radio, Podcasts, and Audiobooks.
- Embellish using music
- Verify the latest weather forecasts
- Follow your investments closely.
- Manage your dwelling
- Make use of a WiFi-enabled app that wasn't developed in-house

Watch relies on your iPhone for several wireless features and connects to it using Bluetooth® wireless technology. Your Watch can automatically set up Wi-Fi networks and connect to those you've already set up or joined using your attached iPhone.

Connect Your Watch To A Cellular Service

Without needing your iPhone or a Wi-Fi connection, the cellular Watch allows you to make and receive calls, send and receive messages, utilize Walkie-Talkie, listen to music and podcasts, get alerts, and more using the same carrier you use for your iPhone.

Cellular coverage and availability vary by location and provider.

Upgrade Your Mobile Plan
Upgrade your mobile plan to include a Watch.

If you follow the on-screen prompts while setting up your Watch, you'll be able to add cellular connectivity. To activate the service at a later time, please do the following:

1. Get out your iPhone and launch the Watch app.
2. Choose Cellular from the My Watch menu.

Control The On/Off Status Of Your Phone

If your iPhone is close, your Watch will utilize that device's cellular connection; otherwise, it will use the Wi-Fi network to which your iPhone is already connected. To save battery life, you have the option to disable cellular data. Here's what you need to do:

1. To access the Control Center, press and hold the bottom of the screen.
2. You may toggle Cellular on and off by tapping its dedicated button.

When your Watch is connected to the internet through cellular data and your iPhone isn't in range, the Cellular button will illuminate in green.

Using cellular for longer periods reduces battery life (see the Watch General Battery Information website for more information). Several applications also need to be connected to your iPhone for updates.

Verify the quality of your mobile signal.

When using a mobile data connection, try one of the following:

- Choose the Explorer watch face, which displays cellular signal strength as a green dot pattern. The effective link size is four dots. Poor quality at only one dot.

- Launch the Command Center. The strength of your cellular connection is shown by the green bars on top.
- Embedding a Cellular complication within the watch face.

Track your data use on the go.

1. Launch the Watch's Settings menu.
2. Choose Cellular, and then scroll down to see your data used for the current billing cycle.

CHAPTER SIX

WATCH'S SECURITY FEATURES

If you're ever in need, your Watch may come in handy.

- Create a Medical ID that shows on the lock screen of your Watch to display vital medical information. The information shown includes your age, blood type, medical problems, and allergies in the event of an emergency.
- Get in touch with the local authorities: To initiate an emergency call, utilize Siri or Messages by pressing and holding the side button on your Watch. Put in your emergency contacts so that they may be notified if anything happens to you.
- Notify emergency personnel of a heavy fall: With Fall Detection on, your Watch may contact emergency services if it detects that you've fallen.
- If of a major vehicle accident, call 911 immediately: In the event of a serious vehicle accident, your Watch Series 9 or Watch SE (2nd Generation) may be able to assist notify emergency personnel.

See & Manage Your Medical Id Card

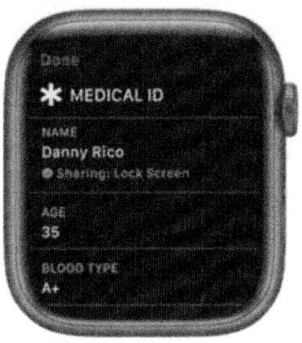

Name, age, and blood type are shown on the Watch's Medical ID screen. A tick appears next to the user's name on the lock screen, indicating that they have been granted permission to share their Medical ID. There is a Finish button in the upper left corner.

You may carry vital information about yourself, such as allergies and medical issues, on a Medical ID in case of an emergency. The medical ID data you enter into the Health app on your iPhone will sync with the Watch. When you use 911 or Emergency SOS on your iPhone or Watch, if you've shared your Medical ID, emergency personnel will be able to access your health information (U.S. and Canada only).

Your Medical ID may be displayed on your Watch, making it easily accessible to first responders.

You may access your Health ID on your Watch by doing the following:

1. To bring up the sliders, press and hold the side button for a few seconds.
2. Turn on Medical ID by moving the toggle to the right.
3. After you're done, press the done button.

In addition, you may access this information by launching the Watch Settings app and navigating to SOS > Medical ID.

Use Your Watch To Get In Touch With 911
Use your Watch to swiftly contact emergency services in a time of need.

If You Are In Danger, Call 911
Choose one of the options below:

- When the display slider is on (by holding the side button), move the Emergency Call slider to the right.

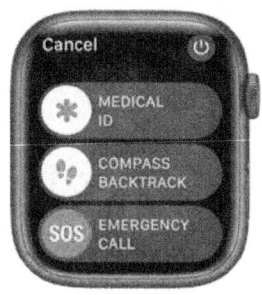

The Watch has three sliders: "Medical ID," "Compass Backtrack," and "Emergency Call". The top right corner has the on/off switch.

> If an emergency occurs, your Watch will contact the appropriate authorities, such as 911 in the United States. (In certain countries, dialing a specific number may be necessary to finish your call.)

- Hold the side button until an alarm and countdown show on your Watch. After the countdown, your Watch will notify authorities. The Emergency Call slider lets you call for assistance without the watch ticking down if you're in trouble.
You may disable Automatic Dialing on your Watch to prevent it from dialing a number when you press the side button. Disable Hold Side Button by pressing SOS in Watch's Settings, then Hold Side Button. Open the iPhone Watch app and navigate to My Watch > Emergency SOS to deactivate Hold Side Button to Dial. In emergencies, the Emergency Call slider is still accessible.
- Just tell Siri "Dial 911."
- To call 911 on your Watch, open Messages, choose New Message, tap Add Contact, then use

the number pad. Tap the Create button, type, and send a message.

After a heavy fall, if your Watch senses that you have remained motionless for roughly a minute, it will try to contact emergency services automatically if you have Fall Detection turned on.

The Watch will notify you and contact 911 within 20 seconds if it detects a significant car crash.

Watch Series 5 (GPS + Cellular), Series 6 (GPS + Cellular), Series 7 (GPS + Cellular), and Series 9 may make emergency calls while in range of a cellular network. Your Watch Series 5, Watch SE, Watch Series 6, Watch Series 7 (GPS + Cellular), or Watch Series 9 may not take an emergency call if it is not enabled, compatible with a certain cellular network, or set up for cellular service.

Your emergency contacts may be preserved. If you don't cancel, your Watch will SMS your emergency contacts after an emergency call. Your emergency contacts are advised of your position changes for a specific period once you activate SOS on your Watch.

When you make an Emergency SOS call abroad, your watch will connect to local emergency services but won't reveal your location or text your emergency contacts. In certain countries and places, you may make international emergency calls without cellular coverage on the watch.

The ability to cancel an emergency call

If you accidentally placed an emergency call, you may terminate it by tapping the End Call button twice.

Make sure your alternate contact information is up to date.

If the emergency services are unable to find you, they will go to the location you designated as your emergency location.

1. Launch the iPhone's Settings menu.
2. To change your emergency contact information, go to Settings > Wi-Fi Calling > Change Emergency Address.

Watch's Fall Detection Can Be Controlled

By activating Fall Detection, the Watch may notify your emergency contacts and call for assistance if it detects a heavy fall. The watch will tap your wrist, sound an alert, and then try to contact emergency services if it senses a heavy fall and determines that you have remained motionless for more than a minute.

If your iPhone 14 or iPhone 14 Pro (or later) is in range of your Watch and cellular and Wi-Fi connectivity is unavailable, the Fall Detection feature on your iPhone will send a notice utilizing Emergency SOS via satellite.

The Safety Monitor for Fall Detection.

If your birthdate is 55 or older, Fall Detection starts immediately when you set up your Watch or attach it to the Health app on your iPhone. The following procedures may be taken by anybody 19–55 to manually activate Fall Detection:

1. Access the Watch's settings using the Settings app.
2. Go to SOS > Fall Detection to activate.

Fall Detection may be enabled in the iPhone Watch app by choosing My Watch, Emergency SOS, and Always On.

If you deactivate wrist detection in the Watch's settings, it won't call 911 after a significant fall.
3. Select "Always on" for constant fall detection, or "Only on during workouts" for activation just after starting an exercise.

For users 19–55, setting up a new Watch with watchOS 9.1 or later allows Fall Detection during workouts. Updating an older Watch to the current OS involves enabling heavy fall detection only during workouts.

Not all falls can be detected by Watch. High-impact activities, which may fool Fall Detection into thinking someone has fallen, become more often as one becomes more physically active.

Control Watch's Collision Detection System
If you're in a major car accident, your Watch Series 9 or Watch SE (2nd Generation) can call 911 and notify loved ones.

Your Watch will notify you of a catastrophic car accident and call 911 after 20 seconds if you don't cancel. If you cannot communicate after an accident, emergency officials will get an audio message describing the severity of the crash, your latitude and longitude, and a proposed search area.

If cellular and Wi-Fi connection is lost and your iPhone 14 or iPhone 14 pro or later is near to your Watch, Emergency SOS via satellite may send Crash Detection notifications to emergency services.

If a significant car crash is detected, Crash Detection won't cancel emergency calls.

Choose whether or not to use Crash Detection.

As a safety measure, Crash Detection is always on. In the event of a serious automobile accident, you may disable Apple's warnings and automated emergency calls by following these procedures:

1. Go into the Watch's settings by using the Settings app.
2. Call after Severe Crash may be disabled by going to SOS > Crash Detection.

Not all automotive accidents can be detected by the Watch.

Activating Voiceover On Your Watch

Even if you can't see the screen on your Watch, you can still utilize it with the aid of VoiceOver. You may navigate the interface with gestures and hear VoiceOver read out your choices.

Adjust The Volume Of The Voiceover

1. Launch the Watch's Settings menu.
2. Start using VoiceOver by selecting Settings > Accessibility > VoiceOver.

   Double-tap the VoiceOver button to disable the feature.

   Tell Siri to toggle VoiceOver on or off.

Instead, you may activate VoiceOver on your Watch by opening the Watch app on your iPhone, selecting My Watch, navigating to Accessibility, and finally selecting the VoiceOver option. Use the Accessibility Shortcut instead.

While setting up, use VoiceOver.

To activate VoiceOver when setting up your Watch, press and hold the Digital Crown three times.

Gestures Used With The Voiceover System

If you're using VoiceOver on your Watch, you can operate it using these movements.

The Always on Display works with VoiceOver. When you tap the screen when it's dark, VoiceOver will zero in on the item you touched.

- Dig into the display: To hear the names of the things you touch on the screen readout, you may move your finger across the screen. The use of a single-finger touch is supported, as is the use of a single-finger swipe to pick a neighboring object. To navigate between pages, use two fingers to swipe left, right, up, or down.
- To go back if you've accidentally taken a wrong turn, you may perform the "two-finger scrub" gesture, which consists of tracing a "z" shape with two fingers on the screen.
- To take action, double-tap an item instead of tapping it once while using VoiceOver to launch an app, toggle a setting, or conduct any other operation. It just takes one touch or swipes to choose an app, list item, or option switch, and a second press to activate it. You may disable VoiceOver in several ways, such as by double-tapping anywhere on the screen after tapping the VoiceOver button.

- To take further measures, listen for the phrase "actions available" whenever you choose an object that has more than one action. To choose an option, swipe up or down, and then double-tap to carry it out.
- To pause reading, use two fingers to touch the screen. This will cause VoiceOver to pause. To continue, use two fingers to tap the screen once more.
- Double-tap and hold with two fingers, then drag up or down to adjust the VoiceOver volume. Instead, you may use VoiceOver by opening the Watch app on your iPhone, selecting My Watch, and then tapping Accessibility > VoiceOver.

The Voiceover Dial

The rotor allows you to quickly navigate between on-screen options and alter VoiceOver preferences. Watch's rotor lets you choose between Words, Characters, Actions, Headings, Volume, and Speech Rate.

To adjust the volume of VoiceOver, use two fingers to spin the screen like a dial. The rotor speed is announced by voiceover. Just keep circling your finger around to discover more customization options. Don't keep turning your fingers till you find the right volume.

To use the rotor, mimic these hand motions.

Action	Gesture
Choose a rotor setting	Rotate two fingers
Move to the previous item or increase (depending on the rotor setting)	Swipe up
Move to the next item or decrease (depending on the rotor setting)	Swipe down

Alter Voiceover's Preferences

The Watch may be used to make changes to VoiceOver's actions. Accessibility > VoiceOver may be accessed via the Settings app on your Watch.

- Stop using VoiceOver.
- Modify your pace of speech
- Turn up or down the VoiceOver.
- Change your Speech Settings
- Just choose Speech and then tweak the voice, pitch, and rotor language settings as needed.
- Alter the haptic experience by activating or deactivating it.
- Activate Braille preferences

  After you've selected Braille, you'll be able to tweak settings like the alert display timeout, the number of seconds Braille is shown, the word wrap, and the Braille tables.

- Options for Keyboards (for Watch Series 7 and Watch Series 9)

  Connect a Bluetooth keyboard to Watch, go to Settings > Keyboards, and adjust the settings for phonetic feedback, typing feedback, modifier keys, keyboard interaction time, and devices.

- To disable VoiceOver suggestions,
- Use the Digital Crown for Navigation
- Raise your wrist to hear the highlighted item's name.
- For more discretion when using VoiceOver, activate Screen Curtain.
- Time allotted for speech: 60
- Set Up Gestures Using Your Hands

Your iPhone also has access to the same settings. Launch the Watch app on your iPhone, choose My Watch, and then go to Accessibility > VoiceOver.

Use Voiceover To Set Up Your Watch

Set up your Watch and connect it to your iPhone with the aid of VoiceOver. A user may activate VoiceOver by touching and holding the screen and then swiping left or right. When anything is highlighted, double-tap to select it.

Set Up Your Watch

1. Keep holding the side button to activate your Watch if it isn't already (below the Digital Crown).
2. To activate VoiceOver on your Watch, just triple-click the Digital Crown.
3. Thus, get your iPhone close to your Watch.
4. Double-tap Continue on your iPhone to proceed.
5. Double-tap the "Set Up Watch" icon on your iPhone.
6. Just hold the iPhone camera approximately a foot away from the watch to check out automatic pairing.

    If you hear a confirmation tone, it means the pairing has been successful. Manual pairing is an option if you're having trouble; just repeat steps 7-13.

7. If you want to manually pair your iPhone with your Watch, go to Settings > General > Watch > Pair Watch.
8. Double-tap the Info button in the Watch's lower-right corner.
9. The Watch ID menu is located toward the top of the screen. You overhear your Watch's identification, which sounds like "Watch 52335".

10. With the iPhone, double-tap this same identifier to pick it.
11. To hear the 6-digit pairing code, choose it on your Watch.
12. Use the iPhone's keyboard to enter the pairing code shown on your Watch.

After the connection is complete, you'll feel a tap on your Watch and hear, "Your Watch is linked." If the pairing attempts fail, press the notifications to reply. If you reset your Watch, the Watch software on your iPhone will also reset, giving you a fresh start.

13. By double-tapping on the Watch app, you may restore it from a backup or set it up as a brand-new device on your iPhone.
14. To proceed with setting up your Watch, just listen to the voice instructions.

After you're done setting up the Watch, it will sync with your iPhone. It will take a few minutes, but you can check on the status by tapping Sync Progress on your iPhone. As soon as you hear "sync complete," your Watch is fully charged and ready to be used. The functions of the watch face may be seen by swiping left or right.

Use Your iPhone To Manage Your Watch

The iPhone's larger display may help those with restricted mobility utilize a Watch. Watch Mirroring lets users utilize the iPhone's accessibility features like Voice Control and Switch Control to interact with their Watch and accept inputs other than touching the display, such as voice commands, sound actions, head tracking, or Made for iPhone switches.

The Watch Series 6, 7, and 9 support Watch Mirroring.

1. To access the preferences menu, use the Settings app on the associated iPhone.
2. To activate Watch Mirroring, go to Settings and then Accessibility and tap the Watch Mirroring toggle.

The iPhone screen takes on a similar appearance to the Watch. Just make movements toward your reflection.

- You may scroll the screen by swiping your finger up or down.
- To switch between displays, just swipe the screen to the left or right.
- Activate the Digital Crown by touching the crown icon on the screen.

- To activate, press the side button: To use, press the screen's side button.
- Tap and hold the Digital Crown on the screen to activate Siri.

Manage Adjacent Electronics

If you have a Watch and an iPhone, your Watch can also operate your iPhone or iPad.

1. Launch the Watch's Settings menu.
2. Choose Accessibility > Nearby Device Control.

   Both devices must be on the same network and have the same Apple ID logged into iCloud.

3. If more than one device is in the area, choose one before tapping the button.

   The buttons have the same functions as the ones on your smartphone.

   - Press the Home Button
   - App Swapper
   - Message Dispensing Hub
   - Command and Conquer
   - Siri
   - Options (includes motions for controlling playback and other media)

If you have VoiceOver enabled on your Watch and you use it to operate a nearby device, VoiceOver will also be activated on that device, and the motions you make on your Watch will be carried out on the device.

Switch Control buttons display on your watch similarly when activated on a nearby device (Move, Next, and Select buttons, for example).

Watch's Assistive Touch Feature

If you have trouble touching the screen or tapping the buttons on your Watch, AssistiveTouch may assist you. The built-in sensors of the Watch allow you to do a variety of tasks, such as picking up a phone call, moving a pointer on a screen, or opening a menu, with a wave of your hand.

AssistiveTouch enables you to do the following steps and more with the use of gestures:

- Toggle the screen by tapping it
- Just by pressing and rotating the Digital Crown,
- Slide between windows on your device.
- Keep your finger on the side button
- Go to the Dock, the Control Center, and the Notification Center.
- Display applications

- Get in on Apple Pay
- Double-clicking the side button is confirmed.
- Use the Siri activation command.
- Start a Siri quick-start routine

Connect Assistive touch

1. Launch the Watch's Settings menu.
2. To activate AssistiveTouch, go to Settings and then Accessibility.
3. Choose Hand Gestures from the menu and toggle it on.

Tap "Learn more" underneath the Hand Gestures switch, then touch each motion, to get a description of how to use it. To learn and master a gesture, just touch it and a short animation will play to guide you.

AssistiveTouch may also be activated through the iPhone app for the Watch by selecting My Watch, then Accessibility, and finally AssistiveTouch.

Assistive touch With The Watch

If you have AssistiveTouch and Hand Gestures enabled, you may use the following movements to control your Watch:

- Forward pinch
- Using a double pinch maneuver:

- Tense: Clench
- Clamp down twice to bring up the context menu

Follow these instructions to utilize AssistiveTouch with the Weather app, for instance, when the Meridian watch face is active:

1. With AssistiveTouch, a double clench is required.

   The Calendar complications get a spotlight treatment.

2. The Temperature conundrum may be accessed by pinching, and tapping it requires a clenched fist.
3. When the Weather app launches, a single click will toggle between the temperature and the current weather.
4. For the Air Quality section, squeeze once to scroll down, and for the UV Index section, pinch again.
5. To return to Air Quality, just double-tap the screen.
6. You may bring up the Action Menu by doing a double-click.
   The activities may be navigated ahead by pinching the screen, and backward by double-tapping.

7. The watch face may be accessed again by selecting the Press Crown action and giving it a firm grip.

Use The Pointer In Motion

The Motion Pointer allows you to interact with your Watch in several different ways, including by tilting the watch up and down and side to side in addition to pinching and clenching. Follow these instructions to utilize the Motion Pointer with the Activity app:

1. To enable AssistiveTouch, double-clench with the watch face up and Watch in list view.
2. To access the Action Menu again, double-click, then pinch to find the Press Crown action and click to activate it.
3. If the Activities app isn't currently open, you may open it by pinching or double-pinching to navigate ahead or return to it.
4. The Interaction action is selected by pinching the screen until it appears and then tapping by clenching twice.

   The choice of the "Motion Pointer" is recommended.
5. The Motion Pointer may be activated by clenching.

The screen now displays a cursor.

6. You may scroll down the screen by tilting your watch so that the pointer is at the bottom. Swipe in from the right side to access the Sharing screen.
7. You can "tap" a button by keeping the cursor over it for a few seconds.
8. Clenching twice will bring up the Action Menu, where you may pinch to pick the Press Crown action and then clench to touch it, bringing you back to the watch face.

Do things quickly

When your Watch displays an alert, you may take immediate action to deal with it. Incoming calls, for instance, will trigger a popup informing you that you may double-pinch to answer the call. In addition to starting a workout when the Watch recognizes exercise-like behavior, pausing an alarm, or stopping a timer, fast actions may now be used to snap a picture when the Camera app's viewfinder and shutter buttons are shown. These are the procedures to take if you want to enable or disable fast actions.

1. Launch the Watch's Settings menu.

2. Choose an action from the Quick Actions menu in the Accessibility menu.

   You have the option of always having access to fast actions, restricting their use to when AssistiveTouch is enabled, or disabling them altogether. You have the option of a full appearance (a banner displays and the action button is highlighted) or a minimal one (the action button is highlighted with no banner).

Quick Actions Gesture Practice Tip: Tap "Try it out"

Modify Your Assistive Touch Options

You may customize the Motion Pointer's sensitivity as well as the movements associated with pinching, clenching, and the Motion Pointer.

Accessibility > AssistiveTouch may be found in the Settings menu of your Watch.

- The motions may be personalized by selecting Hand Gestures, tapping a gesture, and then selecting an activity or Siri shortcut.
- To modify the Motion Pointer, tap Motion Pointer and then change the sensitivity, activation duration, movement tolerance, and hot edges.

- You may choose between Automatic or Manual scanning, wherein activities are highlighted sequentially or individually, respectively.
- Increasing the highlight's visibility requires activating High Contrast in the appearance settings. To change the highlight color, tap the Color button.
- Personalize the menu by adding shortcuts, resizing the Action Menu, and modifying the auto-scroll speed.
- Switch on AssistiveTouch confirmation if you want to utilize it whenever you need to double-click the side button to confirm a purchase or enter a password.
- Accessibility > AssistiveTouch may also be accessed via the Watch app on the iPhone by selecting My Watch > Accessibility > AssistiveTouch.

Zoom In On Your Watch

Use the Zoom function to see more detail on your Watch screen.

Turn on Zoom

1. Go to the Watch's Settings menu and toggle on the Zoom feature.

2. To enable Zoom, choose "Accessibility" from the menu.

Zoom may also be activated remotely through the iPhone, by opening the Watch app, selecting My Watch, tapping Accessibility, and finally selecting Zoom. Instead, you may utilize the Accessibility Shortcut.

Management of Magnification

When Zoom has been activated, the following tasks may be performed via the wrist-worn device.

- To zoom in or out, just use two fingers to double-tap the screen of your Watch.

  If you want a closer look while you're setting up your Watch, try double-tapping with two fingers.

- To pan the view, just use two fingers to drag the screen. The Digital Crown may be used to scroll the full page, left to right and up and down. The position on the page is shown by a little Zoom button.
- If you'd rather not pan with the Digital Crown, you may revert to using it as usual without Zoom enabled by tapping the screen once with two fingers (for example, to scroll a list or zoom a map).

- Change the zoom level: If you double-tap and hold with two fingers, you may then drag your fingers up or down the screen. Adjust the maximum zoom level by using the plus or minus button.

Watch's haptic feedback makes it easy to tell time

The Watch can silently tap out the time on your wrist in a sequence of individual taps. Carry out these steps:

1. Launch the Watch's Settings menu.
2. Choose Taptic Time by pressing Clock and then scrolling down.
3. Launch Taptic Time and choose your preferred display mode, from Digits, Terse, and Morse code. Time is denoted as follows, in both hours and minutes:
    - During the hours, the Watch double-taps every 10 hours, single-taps every hour afterward, double-taps every 10 minutes thereafter, and single-taps every minute thereafter.
    - Sparse: Every five hours, your Watch will make a long tap, then every hour and a half

will make a short tap, and finally every quarter of an hour will make a long tap.
- Watch displays the time in Morse code by tapping out each number.
4. You may get a haptic representation of the time by touching and holding two fingers on the watch's face.

With the Always on Display turned off, Taptic Time continues to function normally.

Taptic Time on the iPhone may also be customized. To activate Taptic Time, launch the Watch app on your iPhone, choose My Watch, then Clock > Taptic Time.

If you've had your Watch configured to constantly read the time out loud, you won't be able to use Taptic Time. Taptic Time requires Control with Quiet Mode to be enabled in Settings > Clock > Speak Time.

CHAPTER SEVEN

CUSTOMIZE THE SIZE OF TEXT

To make it simpler to use the on-screen elements, you may change the font size and other settings.

Modify The Font Size

1. To do so, touch and hold the screen's bottom, and then swipe up.
2. Use the Digital Crown to make the text larger or smaller by tapping the Change Text Size button.

Modify The Layout Of Text

You may customize the look of the screen in several ways, like making text bold, switching to grayscale, and so on. You may toggle the following features on or off in the Accessibility section of the Settings app on your Watch.

- Turn-On/Off Tags

  If you want to show the labels of the buttons in addition to their positions, you may do so by activating this option. When labels are enabled, you'll see a one (1) next to an enabled option and a zero (0) next to a disabled one.

- Grayscale

- Lessen the visibility

  For certain backdrops, readability is improved by decreasing transparency.

- Italicized words

To modify the Watch accessibility settings, launch the Watch app on your iPhone and go to My Watch > Accessibility.

A restart of your Watch is required for the bold and grayscale adjustments to take effect.

Restriction on animation

The Home Screen and app transitions may be slowed down to a crawl.

1. Launch the Watch's Settings menu.
2. To enable Reduce Motion, go to Accessibility > Reduce Motion.

Reduce Motion may also be activated from the iPhone app by selecting My Watch > Accessibility > Reduce Motion > Reduce Motion.

If you choose to Reduce Motion and grid view for the Home Screen, all of your app icons will be the same size.

Set Up And Use RTT On The Watch

For instantaneous communication, there is a system called real-time text (RTT) that sends sound with text. Watch with cellular allows those with hearing or speech impairments to use RTT to communicate when apart from their iPhone. With the Watch app, you can set up Software RTT, so your watch can make phone calls without needing a phone.

Not all carriers and areas enable RTT. In the event of an urgent phone call in the United States, Watch will transmit specific characters or tones to notify the operator. The operator's reception and response to these tones may be affected by factors such as your location. Apple makes no assurances that an RTT call will be received or answered by the operator.

Awaken RTT

1. Get out your iPhone and launch the Watch app.
2. To activate RTT, tap My Watch, then choose Accessibility > RTT.
3. For RTT relay calls, choose Relay Number and input the desired phone number.
4. Switch to the Sending Mode As soon as you input a character, it will be sent. Disable the option to wait until all messages are completed before sending.

Bring on the RTT call

1. To use the phone features of your Watch, launch the Phone app.
2. Choose "Contacts" from the menu, and then use the Digital Crown to browse.
3. Choose the desired contact, swipe down, and then hit the RTT key to initiate a call.
4. To communicate, you may either type a message or choose a prewritten one from a selection, or you can use emojis.

   Scribble isn't translated into every language.

   Messages-style text displays on the Watch.

An alert will sound if the other party in the call does not have RTT enabled.

Accept a Reverse Triangular Call

1. Raise your wrist whenever you hear or feel a call alert so you can see who is calling.
2. Choose "Answer," "Scroll Down," "RTT," and "Answer" to proceed.
3. To communicate, you may either type a message or choose a prewritten one from a selection, or you can use emojis.

   Scribble isn't translated into every language.

Change the canned responses

You may quickly respond with a tap while making or receiving RTT calls on Watch. Here's how you can make more of your responses:

1. Get out your iPhone and launch the Watch app.
2. Choose Default Responses by tapping My Watch, then Accessibility, and finally RTT.
3. Just touch "Add reply," type in your response, and then hit "Done" when you're through.

   A common convention for ending a reply is the letter "GA," which stands for "go ahead" and indicates that you are ready to receive the other person's response.

The Edit button on the Default Answers page allows you to make changes to current responses, remove replies entirely, or rearrange their placement.

Set Watch For Accessible Listening

By activating Mono Audio, you may hear a merged left/right signal from the Watch's speakers or headphones. The audio on your Watch may be adjusted for left/right balance regardless of whether it is stereo or mono. As a bonus, AirPods' accessibility settings are very customizable.

Adjust the volume and balance for mono sound.

To adjust your Watch's hearing features, open the Settings app, choose Accessibility, and then select Hearing.

- Change the sound from stereo to mono by selecting Mono Audio.
- Set the volume level properly: Choose between Left and Right under Mono Audio.

By accessing the Watch app on your iPhone, selecting My Watch, tapping Accessibility, and then turning on Mono Audio, you may fine-tune the volume.

Altering Airpods' Preferences

The AirPods you use with your Watch include options for press speed and press-and-hold length. By wearing one AirPod in just one ear, you may activate noise cancellation on AirPods Pro.

1. Launch the Watch's Settings menu.
2. To adjust your AirPods' accessibility features, tap the menu button and then pick AirPods under the Accessibility menu.

Accessibility > AirPods is also available via the Watch app on the iPhone by tapping My Watch.

Playback Of Homepod Transcripts

If you use the same Apple ID on your HomePod and Watch, your Watch will display text versions of any announcements made by your HomePod.

1. Launch the Watch's Settings menu.
2. To enable audio transcriptions, go to the Accessibility settings.

Activate Watch's Accessibility Functions

Activate Watch's Accessibility Functions With The Help Of Siri

Several of the Watch's accessibility capabilities may be activated with a simple command to Siri. Siri can be used to launch applications, toggle several settings on and off, and serve as a very competent personal assistant.

Siri, say "Turn on VoiceOver" or "Turn off VoiceOver" to activate or deactivate the feature, respectively.

If you have VoiceOver enabled, Siri will be able to read you more information than what is shown. Siri's on-screen text may be read aloud with VoiceOver, too.

Siri's silence interval is fully customizable.

1. Launch the Watch's Settings menu.
2. Choose Siri, then scroll down to the Siri Pause Time section, then touch Default, Longer, or Longest.

Replace spoken requests with text messages while using Siri.

Siri can be used without having to talk to it. Here's how to write Siri commands instead of speaking them.

1. Launch the Watch's Settings menu.
2. Turn on Type to Siri by selecting it from the Accessibility menu and then Siri.

The Watch Accessibility Shortcut

If you choose, you may program a triple-click of the Digital Crown to activate or deactivate the following accessibility options: You can use features like AssistiveTouch, Control nearby Devices, Left/Right Balancing, Decrease Motion, Reduce Transparency, Touch Accommodations, VoiceOver, or Zoom to make things easier.

Configure the Quick Access Menu

1. Launch the Watch's Settings menu.
2. Choose one or more shortcuts under the Accessibility menu.

The Watch app on the iPhone may also be accessed in this way: launch it, then hit My Watch, go to Accessibility > Accessibility Shortcut, and finally choose a preference.

Don't waste time; take the fast way

1. Quickly press the Digital Crown three times. Choose an option to activate or deactivate from the available options if the shortcut has been programmed to do so, and then press the done button to apply your selection.
2. To disable accessibility, repeat the previous step and triple-click the Digital Crown once again.

Restart Your Watch

If your Watch and iPhone aren't functioning properly, you might try rebooting them.

Reboot your Watch

- Get rid of your Watch: Long-press the side button until the sliders appear, then push the Power Button and move the Power Off slider to the right.
- To activate your Watch, press and hold the side button until you see the Apple logo.

The Watch cannot be restarted while it is charging.

Force the iPhone to restart in pairing mode.

- To power down your iPhone, press and hold the side button and a volume button, then move the slider to the right, if you have a Face ID-enabled model. To activate the slider on older iPhone models without Face ID, press and hold the side or top button until it displays, and then swipe it to the right. Settings > General > Shut Down is likewise available on all models.
- Press the side or top button until the Apple logo shows, and your iPhone will power on.

Stop Watch and restart it forcefully

The Watch may need to be restarted manually if you are unable to switch it off or if the issue persists after that. Only try this if restarting your Watch has failed.

To do a hard reset, press and hold the side button and the Digital Crown simultaneously for at least 10 seconds, or until the Apple logo displays.

Discard Watch

If you've forgotten your Watch's passcode, for instance, erasing it could be the only option.

Wipe the Watch and all associated settings

1. Launch the Watch's Settings menu.
2. Choose Wipe All Content and Settings from the General > Reset menu, and then enter your passcode to confirm.

   With a Watch and a cellular data plan, you may choose between two options: Wipe All or Erase All and keep the Plan. Choose Wipe All to permanently delete all data from your Watch. Choose Wipe Everything & Maintain Plan if you need to delete everything but wish to keep your current mobile phone plan.

If you'd rather use your iPhone, open the Watch app, choose My Watch, then General > Reset, and finally press Wipe Watch Content and Settings.

If you've forgotten your Watch's passcode but still need to change certain settings, you may do it by charging the device and then pressing and holding the side button until the sliders show in the Settings app. You may reset your device by pressing and holding the Digital Crown and selecting the option.

This method of erasing the Watch also triggers an Activation Lock, so be aware. If your Watch is ever lost or stolen, you may safeguard it from unauthorized use with the help of the Activation Lock function.

When the reset is complete and the Watch has restarted, you will need to re-pair it with your iPhone by opening the Watch app on your iPhone and then following the on-screen prompts.

Stop paying for a mobile phone contract

You may cancel your Watch's cellular service at any moment.

1. Get out your iPhone and launch the Watch app.
2. Choose "My Watch," then "Cellular," and finally "Info" next to your cellular plan.
3. Choose the carrier from the list, then tap Delete Plan.

    Remove this Watch from your cellular plan by contacting your service provider.

Recover A Watch From A Previous Backup

Backing up to your iPhone is a routine process, and you can easily recover your Watch from a previous backup. When you back up your iPhone to iCloud or your computer, the Watch is backed up as well. You can't access the data in your iCloud backups unless you delete them first.

It's easy to create a backup and restore your Watch.

- Watch data backup: Once a Watch is linked to an iPhone, the information on both devices is automatically and continually backed up to the iPhone. Before you can unpair your devices, however, a backup must be made.
- If you lose your Watch and later find it, or buy a new one, you may restore it from a previous backup by selecting "Restore from Backup" on your iPhone and then choosing the backup you want to use.

When a managed Watch is charged and linked to the owner's Wi-Fi network, it will automatically back up to the owner's iCloud account. By opening the Settings app on the managed Watch and navigating to [account name] > iCloud > iCloud Backups, the user may stop iCloud backups for the watch.

Software Updates Your Watch

If there are any new software updates for your Watch, you may get them through the Watch app on your iPhone.

Ensure that all software is up-to-date and then update it.

1. Get out your iPhone and launch the Watch app.

2. To check for available software updates, open My Watch, touch General, and then tap Software Update.

Instead, you may access Software Update from the General menu in the Settings app on your Watch.

Forget your Watch passcode?

If you have entered an incorrect passcode too many times or have forgotten it, you may use the Watch app on your iPhone to reactivate your Watch. If you have tried everything and still cannot recall your passcode, you may reset your Watch and set it up again.

If you have Wipe Data enabled, your Watch will delete all of its contents after 10 unsuccessful passcode tries.

CHAPTER EIGHT

HOW TO MONITOR YOUR BLOOD OXYGEN LEVELS

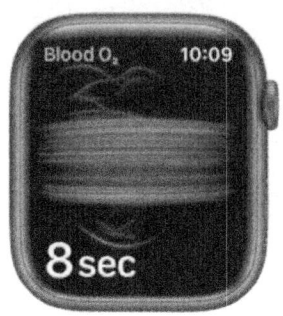

The Blood Oxygen Monitor is taking a reading and the countdown has begun.

To determine how much oxygen your red blood cells are transporting from your lungs to the rest of your body, you may use the Blood Oxygen app on a Watch Series 6 or later. How effectively your blood is oxygenated is a good indicator of your general health.

There is a restriction on the availability of the Blood Oxygen app in certain countries. The results of the Blood Oxygen app should not be used for any kind of medical decision-making.

Provide O2 to the Blood

1. Launch the Watch's Settings menu.
2. Use the Blood Oxygen menu option to activate Blood Oxygen Readings.

While in Sleep Concentration or Theater mode, stop taking readings in the background.

There is a bright red light on the blood oxygen monitor that glows on your wrist; this may be easier to see in low light. If the light from the measures is bothersome, you may disable them.

1. Launch the Watch's Settings menu.
2. To disable In Sleep Focus and Theater Mode, you must first access Blood Oxygen.

Check your blood oxygen level

If background measurements are enabled, the Blood Oxygen app will take readings at set intervals throughout the day; however, you may also take readings whenever you choose by tapping the "Check Now" button.

1. Launch the Watch's Blood Oxygen app.
2. Make sure your wrist is completely flat, with the Watch screen facing up, and then prop up your arm on a table or your lap.

3. Press the Start button, and then keep your arm perfectly motionless for the whole 15 seconds.
4. After the test is complete, you get the results. Finished by tapping.

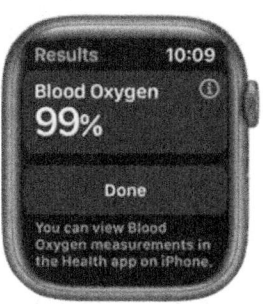

A 99 percent saturation reading for blood oxygen was shown on the screen. There is a Finish button down here.

You must touch your skin with the rear of your Watch. Successful Blood Oxygen readings are more likely to occur when the Watch is worn in a comfortable, but not too loose, fashion that allows the skin to breathe.

Learn about past readings of your blood oxygen level

1. Launch the iPhone's Health application.
2. Start by selecting Browse, then Respiratory, and finally Blood Oxygen.

See And Modify Your Schedule

Watch users may see their upcoming and previous events, as well as those of their contacts, on their wrists using the device's built-in Calendar app. This information is available for the next six weeks and the next two years (in List and Day view). You may pick which calendars to see on your Watch, or view events from all calendars synced with your iPhone.

A screenshot of a calendar displaying the information for a certain event.

Siri: Get your attention with a question like, "When is my next event?"

Check Out Your Schedule On Your Watch

1. Launch the Watch's Calendar app by tapping the date or an event on the watch's face.
2. To see a list of future activities, just turn on the Digital Crown.

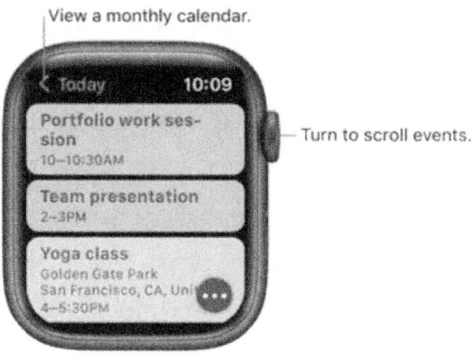

An event list for the current day may be seen on the calendar screen.

3. When you tap an event, further information such as the time, location, attendees, and any notes associated with it will appear.

   A quick touch in the upper left corner will take you to the following function.

Your schedule may be broken down by week or month if you choose.

Alter Your Perspective On Recent Occurrences

The Watch's Calendar app supports many views, and switching between them is as simple as opening the app, tapping the More icon, and selecting a new view.

- Next Up: Displays the week ahead of time.

- Day: Displays just the activities for the current day.
- Timeline: Displays everything happening in your life from the last two weeks to the future two years.

Sliding left or right in Day view will take you to the next day; turning the Digital Crown will take you to List view or Up Next view.

Just tapping the time at the top right of the screen will take you back to the present day and time.

This calendar has a New Event button at the top with Up Next, Day, and List as view choices.

Examining Months and Weeks

You may switch between the week and month views while perusing the calendar in the Day or List view. Launch the Watch's Calendar app and execute one of the following:

- Exhibit this week's schedule: Click the button in the upper left-hand corner.
- To see a different week: The user may choose between a left and right swipe.
- Indicating activities occurring within a certain week: Choose a weekday by tapping on it.
- Display the current month: If you want to see the next week while the current one is shown, press the button in the upper left corner.
- Variable month display: Rotate the Screen Crown Digital.
- Choose any week of the month: Watch the week.

Please insert an event.

The Calendar app on your iPhone will automatically sync with your Watch whenever you add an event. The watch itself may be used to schedule things.

- Make use of Siri: Try: "Add a FaceTime call with Mom on your calendar for May 20 at 4 o'clock"
- If you want to create a new event in Watch's Calendar app, hit the more buttons when in Up Next, Day, or List view. Choose the calendar you'd want to add the event to, give it a name, description, start and finish time, and a list of attendees, and then tap Add.

A new appointment is on the calendar. The event's name appears at the top, followed by a Location text box. There's an "All-day" option in the footer. There is a button labeled "Start Date" at the very bottom.

To modify or eliminate a scheduled activity

- To get rid of a previously made event: Choose the event you want to delete and then touch Delete again.
  You may choose to cancel just this one occurrence or all of them if this is a series.
- To modify an event, use the iPhone's Calendar app.

React to a request made using Calendar

You may react to event invites on your Watch either immediately upon receipt or at a later time.

- After you get the invitation, please check it out. To accept, decline, or maybe the notice, scroll to its very bottom.
- You may find the alert here if you find it later: Choose it in the alerts list, scroll down, and tap to reply.
- Already using Calendar? To react to the event, tap on it.

You may reach the event's organizer using the phone, message, email, or Walkie-Talkie buttons that appear when you press the organizer's name in the event information.

Find your way to a function.

The Watch may lead you to an event's location if one is specified.

1. Get out your Watch and launch the Calendar app.
2. Choose a gathering, then the location, to see it.

Modify the "leave now" messages

If an event specifies a location, your Watch will send you a "leave now" notification depending on how long it'll take you to get there, taking into account any delays due to traffic. The following steps may be taken to zero down on a given time frame, say, two hours before the event:

1. Bring up the Calendar app on your iPhone.
2. Have a listen to the show.
3. Choose a new time frame by tapping Alert.

Modify your schedule accordingly.

Follow these steps to modify the calendar alerts you get and choose which calendars will be shown on your Watch:

1. Get out your iPhone and launch the Watch app.
2. Choose Calendar by selecting My Watch first.
3. Choose Calendars or Notifications and then tap on Custom.

Inquire On A Friend's Whereabouts

The Locate People app is a handy tool for tracking down and notifying the people who matter most about your current whereabouts. To easily find where friends and family are, a map will populate with their whereabouts if they use an iOS device (iPhone, iPad, iPod touch, Watch Series 4 or later). A notification may be programmed to inform you when certain people, such as friends or relatives, depart or arrive at a specified place.

Your profile in Locate People, complete with a "Share My Location" button.

Put a buddy on your list

1. Activate the Watch's Find People feature.
2. Tap the button labeled "Share My Location" and then scroll down.
3. Choose a contact by tapping the Dictation, Contacts, or Keypad buttons.
4. Choose an available contact method (email or phone).
5. Choose a duration for your location sharing—an hour, the rest of the day, or forever.

When you send a friend your current location, your buddy will be alerted. They are free to tell you where they are if they so want. If your friend has agreed to share their position with you, you may see it in a list or on a map in the Find My app on iOS devices (including iPhone, iPad, iPod touch, and Mac) or the Find People app for Watch.

On the Discover People screen, hit the contact's name, and then tap Stop Sharing to terminate location sharing.

The Watch's Share My Location feature may be disabled by going to the Settings app, selecting Privacy & Security, and then Location Services.

Check In With Your Pals

1. When you launch the Locate People app on your Watch, you'll be presented with a list of your contacts, along with an estimate of how far away from you each one is. To see more friends, just rotate the Digital Crown.
2. If you tap a friend's name, you'll be taken to a map showing their general position.
3. To get back to your list of friends, tap the triangle in the upper left corner.

Two entries appear on the screen: one for you, and the other for the person whose location you have revealed.

You may also consult Siri. Inquire, "Where is Julie?"

If your buddy has a Watch that supports cellular and is sharing their location but has forgotten their iPhone at home, their whereabouts may still be followed by using the Watch.

You should let a buddy know when you leave or return.

1. Activate the Watch's Find People feature.
2. Choose the contact you want to notify by tapping on their name, scrolling down, and finally selecting the Notify option.
3. If you want to let a friend know when you leave your location or when you arrive at their location, you may do so by activating Notify [name of friend] on the following screen.

Get an alert when a buddy is nearby.

1. Activate the Watch's Find People feature.
2. To send a notification to a friend, touch on them, then on Notify Me.
3. You may opt to be alerted when a buddy leaves their location, arrives, or both by using the Notify Me feature.

Find Your Way, Or Reach Out To A Buddy

You may use Find People to locate a friend instantly.

Find your pal's whereabouts.

1. Activate the Watch's Find People feature.
2. The Maps app may be accessed by tapping your buddy, scrolling down, and then tapping Directions.
3. Get turn-by-turn instructions from your present location to your friend's location by simply tapping the route.

Talk To A Close Pal

1. Activate the Watch's Find People feature.
2. For the option to phone, email, or send a message to the friend in question, hit their profile and then scroll down to the Contact button.

Track Lost Gadgets

Locate Devices is an app for Watch that may be used to track misplaced iOS devices. The only way to locate your misplaced Apple gear is to link it to your Apple ID.

In this screenshot from Apple's Find Devices app, we can see a Watch and a pair of AirPods.

Examine the precise positioning of a gadget.

The Locate Devices app will show you precisely where your internet device is. When used with a compatible device, Locate Devices can pinpoint its location even while the gadget is dormant, in Low Power Mode, or airplane mode.

To locate a specific Watch, use the Find Devices app and choose it from the list.

- You may see exactly where the gadget is in question by checking its location on a map if one is available. Information like as the battery life, the last time the device connected to Wi-Fi or cellular, and its approximate location are shown above the map. Detailed directions are provided below the map.
- If the device cannot be found, "No location" will be shown next to its name. Choose Notify when Found from the Notifications menu. As soon as it's found, you'll get an alert.

Use your Apple device (iPhone, iPad, iPod touch, Mac, Watch) to play an audio file.

1. To locate a specific Watch, use the Find Devices app and choose it from the list.
2. Please press the play button for the audio.
   - Assuming connectivity, if the gadget: After a brief pause, a sound begins and, over two minutes, the level steadily rises until finally peaking. This machine gives forth vibrations (if applicable). Your device will display a "Find My" message to help you locate it.
   A notification will also be sent to the address associated with your Apple ID.
   - Sound Pending appears if the gadget is not connected to the internet. After the smartphone reconnects to a cellular or Wi-Fi network, the sound will play.

Put on your headphones, whether they are AirPods or Beats, and play a sound.

With Locate Devices, you may send a sound to any AirPods or Beats headphones that are associated with your Watch.

For compatible versions of AirPods, you can even hear a sound through the case.

1. To locate a specific Watch, use the Find Devices app and choose it from the list.

2. Choose the Sound Play option. If you have lost one of your AirPods or AirPods Pro, you may silence it by searching for it by swiping left or right.
   - If the gadget is connected to the internet, a sound will play continuously for two minutes. A notification will also be sent to the address associated with your Apple ID.
   - Whenever the gadget comes within range of your Watch after being offline, you will be notified.

Learn how to go to a gadget.

The Watch's Maps app may be used to receive directions from the wearer's present location to any other place.

1. To get instructions for a specific device, launch the Locate Devices app on your Watch and then touch it.
2. Use the "Directions" button to launch Maps.
3. Directions from your present location to where the gadget is may be accessed by tapping the route.

A reminder will appear on your smartphone if you leave it behind.

Whenever you leave your smartphone behind, you can get a notification so you don't lose it. There's also the option to designate some areas as "Trusted Places," where you won't get a warning when you leave your device.

1. Get out your Watch and launch the Find My Devices app.
2. Choose the gadget you want to notify by tapping on it.
3. To enable Notify When Left Behind hit Notify When Left Behind, which can be found under Notifications.

To set up a notice when your iPhone is left behind, open the Find My app, go to Devices, select the device in question, and then hit Notify When Left Behind. Just activate the feature labeled "Alert When Left Behind" and proceed with the on-screen prompts.

To add a Trusted Place, choose one from the drop-down list or press New Location, go to the desired spot on the map, and finally, hit Done.

Put a lost device on the lost list

Lock your Mac, or activate Lost Mode on your iPhone, iPad, iPod touch, or Watch if you think it may have been stolen.

1. To locate a specific Watch, use the Find Devices app and choose it from the list.
2. Choose "Lost Mode" from the menu and activate it.

There are a few things that happen when a gadget is reported lost:

- The email address associated with your Apple ID will get a confirmation message.
- The Lock Screen displays a notification saying the device has been misplaced and providing contact information.
- There are no visual or audible indicators for incoming messages, notifications, or alarms on your smartphone. You can still get the phone and FaceTime calls on your gadget.
- Currently, Apple Pay is not available on your device. Apple Pay debit and credit cards, student IDs, and Express Transit passes are deleted from your device. If your device is offline, you will still be able to have your credit, debit, and student ID cards canceled. If you have an Express Transport card, it will be

automatically deleted the next time your device connects to the internet.
- An iOS device's (iPhone, iPad, iPod touch, or Watchcurrent) position and any changes to that location are shown on a map.

Track Down An Airtag Or Other Object

When you register an AirTag or third-party item with your Apple ID, you may use the Find Items app on your Watch to track it down if you lose it.

With the Locate Things utility, you can prove that your keys, which have an AirTag attached to them, are in your possession.

Check out where something is stored.

You may locate misplaced items by launching the Locate Items app on your Watch and tapping the object in question.

- If the object can be found, its location will show up on the map. Information like as the battery life, the last time the device connected to Wi-Fi or cellular, and its approximate location are shown above the map. Detailed directions are provided below the map.
- If you can't find anything, you may check the last known location and time it was there. To activate Notify When Found, go to the Notifications tab. As soon as it's found again, you'll be notified.

Start a sound effect

The use of audible cues may help locate objects that are close at hand.

The Play Sound button won't appear if the item doesn't support playing sounds.

1. You may assign a sound to any object by opening the Find Things app on your Watch and tapping on it.
2. Choose the Sound Play option.

    You may interrupt the sound's playback by selecting Stop Sound before it finishes automatically.

Find out how to go there

With your Watch and the Maps app, you can receive driving instructions to the current or last known location of an object.

1. To acquire instructions for an item, launch the Locate Items app on your Watch and touch the object in question.
2. Use the "Directions" button to launch Maps.
3. When you tap the route, it will show you how to travel from where you are right now to where the item is kept.

Find out right away whether you've forgotten anything

You may get an alert when you leave anything behind to help you remember where you put it. You may even choose some areas as "Trusted Places," or spots where you can leave your item without worrying about being notified.

1. Swipe up on your Watch to access the Locate Things menu.
2. Choose the content for which you'd want to get alerts by tapping on it.
3. Choose the "Alert When Left Behind" option and toggle it on.

Another option is to launch the Locate My app on your iPhone, go to Items, choose the item for which you'd want to get a notice, and finally, select Notify When Left Behind. Just activate the feature labeled "Alert When Left Behind" and proceed with the on-screen prompts.

To add a Trusted Place, choose one from the drop-down list or press New Location, go to the desired spot on the map, and finally, hit Done.

Report a missing AirTag or other item using Watch's Find Things app.

Put a lost device on the lost list

The Locate Things app lets you report missing AirTags and other third-party items associated with your Apple ID.

1. Choose an item and launch the Locate It app on your Watch.
2. Choose "Lost Mode" from the menu and activate it.

To find out more about your thing, someone only has to connect to it after they've located it.

Disable an item's Lost Mode settings.

As soon as you locate your misplaced object, you should exit Lost Mode.

1. Tap the object, and then launch the Find Things app on your Watch.
2. You may disable Lost Mode by tapping the Lost Mode button.

Use Your Watch To Monitor Your Pulse

Checking your heart rate is a good indicator of your overall health. In addition to seeing your resting, walking, exercise, and post-workout heart rates, as well as your heart rate during a Breathe session, you may also take a fresh reading at any moment.

Keep your wrist and Watch free of dirt and moisture. Moisture from perspiration and other sources may degrade audio recordings.

Take a look at your pulse.

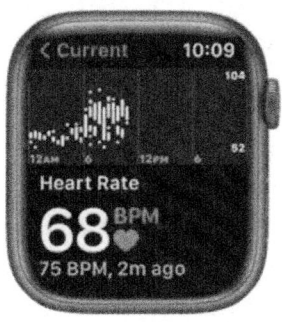

The Heart Rate app's main interface, displays the current time and date in the bottom left corner, the latest reading in smaller print below it, and a chart illustrating your heart rate throughout the day in the upper right corner.

To check your current heart rate, resting heart rate, and walking average rate launch the Heart Rate app on your Watch.

As long as you're wearing your Watch, it will keep tracking your heart rate.

See your heart rate statistics on a graph.

1. Launch the Watch's Heart Rate app.
2. Choose from the three heart rate displays—Current, Resting Heart Rate, and Walking Average—to see your average readings throughout the day.

Open the Health app on your iPhone, choose Browse, then select Heart, and finally select an entry to see your heart rate statistics over a longer period. Whether the data is from the heart's last hour, day, week, month, or year, you may see it all.

Start recording your heart rate

The Watch automatically tracks your heart rate during exercises, Breathe and Reflect sessions, and the Heart Rate app. If you have previously disabled heart rate monitoring, you may enable it again.

1. Launch the Watch's Settings menu.
2. Choose Health > Privacy & Security.
3. The Heart Rate feature may be activated by tapping the Heart Rate icon.

Instead, you may see Heart Rate by opening the Watch app on your iPhone, selecting My Watch, and then Privacy.

Watch Series 6, Series 7, and Series 9 only: The back of your Watch must be in touch with your skin for wrist identification, haptic alerts, and blood oxygen level readings. Comfort and accurate sensor readings come from wearing your Watch in just the right way, which means not too tight, not too loose, and with enough breathing space for your skin.

Medications May Be Tracked On Watch

The Health app on your iPhone is where you can keep track of all the pills, powders, and capsules you consume. You may register your prescriptions and set reminders in the Medications app on your Watch.

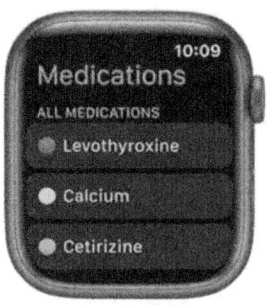

This is a screenshot of the Medications app, which displays a complete list of drugs.

The Medicines function is not meant to replace your doctor's advice. Always check your doctor or pharmacist before making any health-related choices based on the information found on the labels of your drugs.

Manage your prescription regimen with ease using your iPhone.

1. Launch the Medications tab in the Health app on your iPhone by tapping the Browse button in the app's lower right corner.
2. To begin compiling your list of medications, choose Add Medicine (to add to your list).
3. Do one of the following to determine what drug is being used:
    - A name should be typed in: Choose the search bar, type the name, then select Add.

Only in the United States will you get autocomplete recommendations as you type. You may choose a suggested name or type the name in full and then hit Add.

- Use the camera: (Only available in the US on the iPhone SE (2nd gen) and after, the iPhone XS, and the iPhone XR.) Follow the on-screen prompts by tapping the Camera icon to the right of the search bar.

  If no results are returned after a few seconds, choose Search by Name and enter the name (as described above).

4. You may follow the on-screen prompts to make a visual marker, establish a routine, and determine potential interactions.

Prescriptions should be recorded.

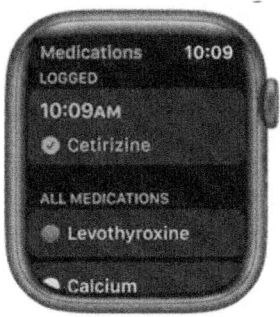

The medication history is shown by the Medicines app.

If you set up a medicine plan in the Health app on your iPhone, your Watch will automatically remind you when it's time to take your pills. These are the actions you need to take to maintain an accurate medication record.

1. A medicine log notice should be tapped if you have received one. In any other case, use the Watch's Medicines app.
2. Review the existing medication regimen, such as the pills you take first thing in the morning.
3. To record all actions taken, choose the corresponding log.

   The watch keeps track of when and how many units of medicine you take.

4. Scroll down, press a medicine under Your Medications, and then choose Log to record only that one.

   Under Logged, you'll see the medication's name and when it was last taken.

5. A medicine's status may be updated by tapping the medication, selecting Taken or Skipping, and then tapping done.

If you have an iPhone, you may access the log and your prescription history by opening the Health app, tapping Browse, and then tapping Medications.

Use Mindfulness With Your Watch

The Watch's Mindfulness app suggests taking a few minutes each day to breathe deeply to relax, refocus, and reconnect. For those who have subscribed to Apple Fitness+, the Watch can play audio tracks that lead you through meditation.

Get some quiet time to think or breathe going.

To practice mindfulness, launch the Mindfulness app on your Watch and choose from the following options:

- Focus your mind by tapping Reflect, reading the topic, and then tapping Begin to start reflecting.
- To breathe, choose to Breathe, and then gently inhale as the animation expands and exhale as it contracts.

Swipe right and then choose End to terminate a session early.

The "Discover something near to you" prompt is a contemplative concept presented by the Mindfulness app. Take note of the specifics. Below, you'll find a Start button.

Determine how long a session will last

1. Launch the Watch's Mindfulness application.
2. The duration may be adjusted by selecting "More Settings," "Duration," and then a specific time frame.

   Anything from one to five minutes is up for grabs.

The Mindfulness app's main screen, with a timer set to one minute shown at the very top. Here are some suggestions for making the most of your Reflect time.

Modify your mind-body settings

You may customize the frequency of reminders, silence them for the day, adjust the pace at which you breathe, and choose your preferred haptic feedback.

Launch the Watch's Settings menu, choose Mindfulness, and then perform one of the following:

- Remind yourself to be present: Choose Start of Day and End of Day under Reminders then press Add Reminder to set further reminders.
- Switch on Weekly Summary to start getting weekly summaries or turn it off to cease receiving them.
- Turn on "Mute for today" to silence today's mindfulness prompts.
- Slow down your breathing: Click the Breath Rate button to set a new rate in breaths per minute.
- To adjust the haptics, choose Haptics and then decide between No Haptics, Some Haptics, and Plenty of Haptics.

- Here's where you may get fresh meditations: While your Watch is plugged into a power source, you may download new meditations by activating the feature called Add New Meditations to Watch. After you finish a meditation, it will be erased from your account automatically.

You can also access this feature by opening the Watch app on your iPhone, selecting My Watch, and then tapping Mindfulness.

Check your pulse while meditating.

Do some deep breathing or a reflective exercise. The Summary page displays your current heart rate.

And remember, your heart rate data is stored for future reference. To check your heart rate, open the Health app on your iPhone, choose Browse, then Heart. Then, press the button labeled See More Heart Rate Data, then swipe up and press the button labeled Breathe.

Get the Breathe watch dial.

When you equip your watch with the Breathe face, you'll have instantaneous access to guided meditations.

1. You may change the watch's face by touching and holding the screen.
2. Tap the New button (+) once you've swiped to the left.
3. To add the Breathe mode, you'll need to turn the Digital Crown to pick it, and then press the Add button.
4. By touching the watch face, you may launch the Mindfulness application.

This watch has the Breathe face.

Enjoy Guided Meditations
With a Watch and an Apple Fitness+ membership, you can listen to guided meditations on the go.

AirPods or other Bluetooth headphones or speakers may be used to listen to guided meditations with Apple Fitness+ and your Watch.

Apple Fitness+ isn't available worldwide.

Do some kind of guided meditation.
1. Launch the Watch's Mindfulness application.
2. Use the Fitness+ Audio Meditations.
3. You may scroll up and down to look at different parts of the meditation.

    Towards the end of each segment, you'll find information on the episode's topic, instructor, and meditation time.

4. You can access the meditation's playlist in the Music app by tapping the Information icon, where you can also find out more about the meditation and add it to your collection.
5. To start meditating, just tap the one you want to use.

Watch will display the duration of the meditation and your current heart rate while it plays.

Once a guided meditation is playing, you may stop it by swiping right, and you can terminate it by doing the same. When the meditation is playing in the background, you may start your exercise by selecting Workout and then a specific routine.

Go over your finished meditations.

After you've finished a whole meditation, it will display in My Library in the Fitness app on your iPhone and Watch.

1. Launch the Watch's Mindfulness application.
2. Listen to Fitness+ guided meditations on your phone.
3. To see previously listened-to meditations, swipe down and choose My Library.
4. To read more about the meditation, add it to your collection, delete it, or listen to its playlist in the Music app, tap the Information icon.
5. The meditative tracks may be replayed by tapping on them.

Your iPhone, iPad, or Apple TV may also be used to peruse your My Library collection. Launch Fitness from your app drawer (iPhone users: choose Fitness+) and go to the "My Library" tab.

Choose A Picture Album
Choose A Picture Album And Handle Space Allocation

With your Watch, you can access your favorite iPhone albums, along with Featured Pictures and Memories.

Pick The Album For Watch

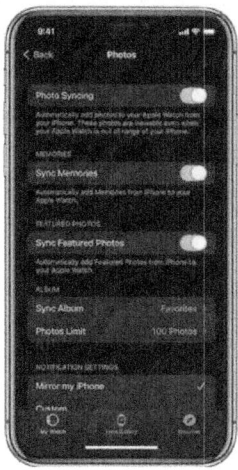

The Watch app on the iPhone allows you to choose the album to save on the Watch Photographs settings, with the Picture Syncing option in the center and the Photos Limit setting below that.

Your Watch will automatically show photographs from the Favorites album (any photos you've marked as favorites) when you first acquire it, but you may modify this if you'd like.

1. Get out your iPhone and launch the Watch app.
2. Choose an album by tapping My Watch, then Sync Album.

When you want to get rid of a picture from your Watch, you may do so by opening the Photos app on your iPhone and erasing it from the album you've synchronized.

Use the Pictures app on your iPhone to create a new album just for images taken with your Watch.

Highlight images and Memories on your Watch.

Featured photographs and Memories may be automatically synchronized from your iPhone's photo library to your Watch.

1. Get out your iPhone and launch the Watch app.
2. Choose My Watch > Photographs > Sync Memories and Sync Featured Pictures to activate.

Put an end to the synchronization of your photos!

Use these steps to prevent your iPhone from syncing photographs from the Memories, featured, or selected albums:

1. Get out your iPhone and launch the Watch app.
2. Choose "My Watch," "Photos," and "Off" to disable syncing of your photos.

Watch picture storage should be restricted.

Depending on the capacity of your Watch, you may only be able to keep a limited amount of images on it. You may reduce the number of pictures saved on it so that more room can be made available for music or other media.

1. Get out your iPhone and launch the Watch app.
2. Choose Photographs > Pictures Limit from the My Watch menu.

One of the following may be done to count the number of pictures on your Watch:

- If you want to check your Watch's history, you may do so by opening the Settings app and then selecting General > About.
- Go to General > About in the Watch app on your iPhone by tapping My Watch.

Open the Settings app on your Watch, then go to General > Storage, to see the percentage of available storage that is being utilized by your photographs. Launch Watch on your iPhone, then touch My Watch, followed by General > Storage.

You should snap a picture of your Watch.

1. To enable screenshots on your Watch, open the Settings app, go to General > Screenshots, and then tap Enable Screenshots.

2. To snap a screenshot, hold down the Digital Crown and the side button at the same time.

When you take a screenshot on your iPhone, it will be stored in the Pictures app.

Examine Snapshots & Recollections
Watch's Pictures app is where you'll go to go through your collection and choose a photo to use as your watch face.

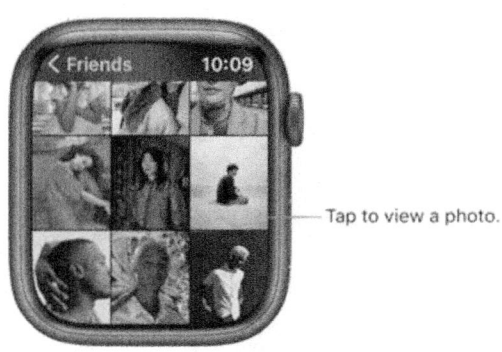
Tap to view a photo.

The home screen of Watch's Pictures app displays a grid of images.

Check out snaps on your Watch via the Pictures app.

These gestures may be used to launch the Pictures app on your Watch and begin looking through your photo library.

1. Choose an image from your iCloud library or Featured Pictures, or choose an album you've synced to your Watch.
2. To check out an image, just tap on it.
3. To navigate between images, swipe left or right.
   - By rotating the Digital Crown, you may zoom in or out and pan around an image.
   - If you want to view the whole picture album, you need to zoom out.

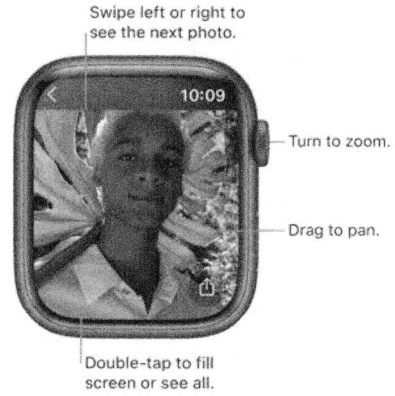

Photos may be navigated by turning the Digital Crown to zoom in or out, dragging to pan around, or double-tapping to toggle between full-screen and normal viewing. Image galleries may be navigated by swiping left or right. On the right-hand corner, there is a Share button.

Check out a snapshot of an experience on your wrist

Besides the Photos app, the Memories feature is now accessible through Siri and Photos watch faces on your Watch.

- One of Siri's latest recollections is shown on the wristwatch's face. Choose the "Siri" watch face, and then select an experience.
- The Photographs watch face displays images from the Memories album. To make the Photographs watch face dynamic, launch the Watch app on your iPhone, go to Face Gallery, and finally hit the Pictures watch face.

The dynamic watch face automatically refreshes with new photographs from your most recent Memories.

Examine a Real-Time Image on Your Watch

Touch and hold the Live Picture symbol in the photo's bottom left corner to view live action.

Post a picture

The Pictures app on the Watch has an Action button that allows you to choose a sharing method while viewing a photo.

Personalize your watch with a picture

You can accomplish this by tapping the Action button while in the Pictures app on your Watch, then scrolling down and tapping Make Face. The Watch software on your iPhone also allows you to make a Kaleidoscope watch face from the picture or add a new Photographs watch face.

Customizing your iPhone's watch face is a breeze. You may make a Portraits, Photographs, or Kaleidoscope watch face by opening the Photos app on your iPhone, tapping a picture, tapping the Action button, swiping up, and tapping Make Watch Face.

Siri, on your Watch, will tell you the forecast if you want to know. Specifically, you may ask, "What is tomorrow's prediction for Honolulu?"

Have A Look At The Forecast

- Check out today's weather and conditions: Launch the Watch's weather application. Choose a city and use your fingertip to swipe through hourly weather, conditions, and temperature predictions.

In-app weather forecast with hourly updates.

- Check out the weather prediction for the next ten days, as well as details on the air quality, UV index, wind speed, humidity, and visibility. Scroll down after tapping a city.

  Choose on the top left to get back to the original list of cities.

The Weather app's list view displays current conditions in two cities.

Not everyone has access to data on the quality of their air.

Modify The Weather Recordings

With the Weather app, you may choose which metric appears under each city's name while browsing a list of cities.

1. Launch the Watch's weather app.
2. Choose Watching from the menu bar.
3. Choose the Temperature, the Precipitation, or the Conditions.

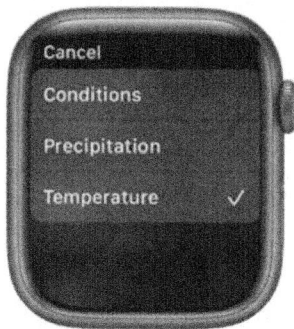

Conditions, Precipitation, and Temperature are the three options shown by the Weather app.

Choose the city you want to be the default.

1. Launch the Watch's Settings menu.
2. Choose a city by tapping the Weather app, then the Default City menu option.

The Watch software on the iPhone may also be accessed by going to the Weather > Default City menu through the My Watch menu.

If you've set your watch to display the weather for a specific location, you may see the current conditions there.

Check for weather updates at the following links:

With the Weather app, there is a warning regarding potential dangers at the beach.

The Weather app may display a warning at the top of the screen if a severe weather event is forecast.

Set & React To Reminders

Any Reminders app reminders on your Watch or iPhone (or any iOS device, iPad, or Mac connected in with your Apple ID) will display as a Watch notification.

Check Your Notes For Upcoming Events
1. Bring up the Reminders app on your Watch.
2. Just tapping a list will reveal its contents.
3. To mark an item as finished, either hit the Reminder Done button on the left side of the screen or tap the reminder itself, followed by Mark as Finished.
4. To get back to the list view, tap the arrow icon in the upper left.
5. To see the checked-off reminders in a list, select the list, choose View Options, and then select Display Completed.

   Choose all from the list, then View Options, and finally Display Completed to get a full history of your reminders.

You may rearrange your lists in Reminders by opening the app, selecting Edit, and then dragging and dropping the list to its new spot on your iPhone.

If you and your collaborators are using iCloud, you may easily share and collaborate using shared lists. The recipients of a particular reminder may be seen in a shared list. You can add someone to an existing shared list, but you can't create a new shared list from your Watch.

Under the Lists tab of the Reminders app, you may choose from the three pre-set lists: Family, Work, and Shopping. The right-hand numbers indicate the total number of reminders in each set of bullets. You may scroll among available lists by rotating the Digital Crown, or you can tap a list to read its contents.

Do action in response to a gentle prodding

- If you check your inbox when the reminder arrives: Mark it as Done or set a reminder by tapping the notice, swiping (or using the Digital Crown to scroll), and then tapping the appropriate option.
- You may find the alert here if you find it later: Choose it in the alerts list, scroll down, and tap to reply.

Set An Alarm To Remind Yourself

An item from the Today list in the Reminders app. The notification appears in the screen's upper-right corner, with an Add Reminder button just underneath it.

- Make use of Siri: The dry cleaning has to be picked up at 5 o'clock, so please remind me of that.
  The Watch's Siri assistant may also be used to compile a list.
- Make a note of it by using the app Reminders: The Add Reminder button may be found at the very bottom of any list.

Get rid of a prompt

1. Bring up the Reminders app on your Watch.
2. You may perform one of the following after tapping a list to open it:

- Tap the Trash icon after swiping left on the reminder.
- Choose the notification, swipe down, and select Delete

Modify A Prompt

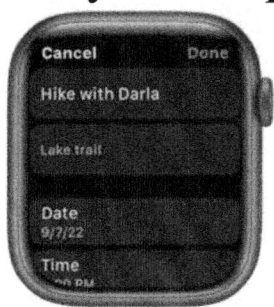

Watch's Reminders app Edit screen. The name of the reminder appears at the top, followed by a brief explanation. The time and date the prompt will appear are mentioned at the bottom. The task may be completed by clicking the done button in the upper right corner.

Reminders that you put up for yourself on your Watch may be managed and updated on the go.

1. Bring up the Reminders app on your Watch.
2. When you touch a list, then a Reminder, or edit, you may perform any of the following:
   - Name the reminder something else by tapping its current name and entering the new name

through the QWERTY and QuickPath keyboard (not available in all languages, Watch Series 7 and Watch Series 9 only), dictation, Scribble, or emoji.

Scribble isn't translated into every language.

- Observe this: Choose the Add Notes option and type your remark.
- Include a time and date: Choose the desired date by tapping the Date tab. To set the time press the Time button, then press AM or PM, then press the hour or minute, and last, spin the Digital Crown.
- Type in a tag: Choose Tags and then either select an existing tag or touch Create New to create a new tag.
- Insert a place name: Choose the place you want to be reminded of anything, such as when you enter a building or a vehicle equipped with Bluetooth that can communicate with your Watch, by tapping Location.
- Send yourself a little nudge to remember to activate Flag.
- Choose a Top Concern: To change the priority level, choose Low, Medium, or High.

- Transfer the nagging thought to a new set of priorities: Choose a List by clicking the List button.

Explore New Areas

You may check out your immediate area and receive driving instructions using the Maps app on your Apple Watch.

Invoke Siri with a phrase like:

- I'm lost.
- Saying, "I need to locate a coffee shop close to me."

Look around the map

1. Launch the Apple Watch's Maps app.
2. To dictate or scribble, press Search, then Dictate or Scribble, respectively. Both the QWERTY and QuickPath keyboards are available on Apple Watch Series 7 and Series 9. (Not available in all languages).

   With the Apple Watch Series 7 and Apple Watch Series 9, you can access Scribble by swiping up from the bottom of the screen and then selecting Scribble.

   Scribble is not translated into all languages.

Find A Close-By Provider

1. Launch the Apple Watch's Maps app.
2. Choose a category, such as "Restaurants" or "Parking," by tapping the List button.
3. Choose a result by tapping it, and then use the Digital Crown to browse the details.
4. To exit back to the results list, tap the arrow icon in the upper left corner.

Nearby recommendations aren't always accessible.

The Search bar is prominently displayed towards the top of the Maps app's Search panel. There are links to COVID-19 vaccinations, local eateries, and quick food joints under the nearby tab.

Examine a manual

1. To execute any of the following, you'll need to launch the Maps app on your iPhone, hit the search box, scroll up, and then:

- Choose a cover to open a guidebook from the City Guides or Guides We Love categories.
- To peruse the available guides, choose Browse Guides and then touch on a cover.
- Choose an option from the list of publishers by tapping its cover.
2. To add a place, such as a park or a restaurant, swipe up and then touch the Add button next to the place's name.
3. Choose an existing guide to update, or create a new one, if appropriate.
4. To access this instruction, launch the Maps app on your Apple Watch, scroll down to find the place you just entered, and touch on it.

Not all areas have access to guides.

View & Investigate The Immediate Area
1. Launch the Apple Watch's Maps app.
2. Find Your Spot.
3. Choose more, then Search Here to search for your current location.

For a visual representation of available public transportation, use the Transit Map button.

Transit Map is not accessible worldwide.

A map is seen in the Maps app. A blue dot will represent your position on the map.

A blue cone appears on the Apple Watch SE and subsequent models' maps to indicate the direction your watch is pointing.

Flip and refocus

- To move the map, just use one finger to drag.
- Use the digital crown to zoom in or out of the map.
  If you double-tap the screen, the map will zoom in on the current location.
- Touch the Location icon in the lower right corner to return to the current place.

Find out more about a well-known spot

1. Choose the pin on the map.
2. You may navigate through the menus by rotating the Digital Crown.

3. Choose on the top left to get back to the map.

Contact the listed phone number. Launch the App Switcher on your iPhone to switch to it. To access the Phone app, slide up from the bottom edge and pause (or double-click the Home button) on an iPhone with Face ID, then tap the button at the bottom of the screen.

Place & Reposition Map Markers

- To place a pin, touch and hold the location on the map until the pin drops into place, then release your finger.
Tap the blue dot, and then press Mark My Place to set a marker at your present location.
- To relocate a pin, just touch and hold it, drag it, or place a new pin where you want it to go.
- Touch the pin to see the address details, scroll with the Digital Crown, and then hit Remove Marker to get rid of it.

With the Maps app, you may acquire directions to a certain location or find out its rough location by tapping the red pin on the map.

A quick way to get the approximate address of any point on the map is to put a pin there and touch on it to bring up the address details.

New Places to Look At

1. Launch the Apple Watch's Maps app.
2. Underneath the Recents section, you'll see a selection of options to tap.

Guides you've recently seen on your iPhone may also be found in Recents.

Find Your Way

Invoke Siri with a phrase like:

- "Where can I find the closest gas station?"
- "Find Driving Directions"
- Inquiring, "How long is it to the airport?"

Find Your Way

1. Launch the Apple Watch's Maps app.
2. The Digital Crown may be used to go to the Most Used, Favorites, and Recents screens.
3. If you tap an entry, you'll see options for getting there by car, on foot, by bus, or by bike.

Not all types of transportation are available in all areas.

After selecting a mode, a list of recommended routes will appear, and you may touch one of them to begin your journey and get an overview of it, complete with arrows, distances, and street names.

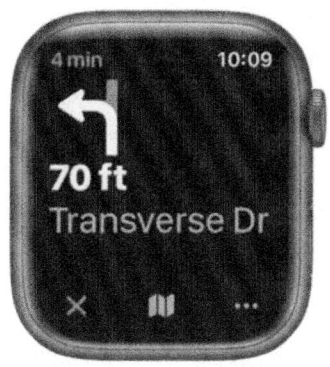

Your expected arrival time is shown in the upper left corner. How much longer you get there may be shown by tapping the arrival time.

The Maps app will display the remaining time, the next turn's street name, and the distance till you reach that turn in the upper left corner. Underneath it are several buttons labeled "End," "Map," and "More."

A summary of the route's elevation changes is shown when the Cycling option is selected. You can find out whether there is a bike path, if it is a side road, a major road, or if you need to get off your bike and walk by tapping more buttons.

Learn Your Travel Alternatives

The Maps app will provide you with recommended routes so you can compare your alternatives before setting off.

- If suggested detours are shown, you may press one to switch to it.
- To choose a different mode of transportation, such as walking, driving, public transportation, or cycling, select the appropriate button.
- When a driving route is shown, you may avoid tolls and motorways by tapping > next to the destination's address and activating the corresponding option.
- With a bike route shown, touch > next to the destination's address, and then toggle on an option to avoid hills or congested highways.
- If a transit route is currently shown, you may choose your chosen mode of public transportation from among bus, subway/light rail, commuter train, and ferry by tapping >.

Find your way to a certain address, intersection, or map point.

The destination is seen by the Maps app. You may find the Stop, List, and more links down here.

1. Launch the Apple Watch's Maps app.
2. Choose the Location and then the desired location on the map.
3. You can select walking, driving, transit, or bicycle routes by scrolling down to the Location Details section.
4. Tap a route when you're ready to go, then follow the on-screen instructions.

Siri, how long would it take me to go home if I leave right now?

Refer to maps when on the road.

Your Apple Watch may assist you in staying on track in a variety of ways. Choose one of these trip choices:

- Learn the specific streets and highways you'll be traveling on using Apple Watch's turn-by-turn guidance. The Digital Crown may be turned to preview forthcoming turns, and a touch at the top of the screen will transport you back to the next turn you'll be taking.
Location services must be enabled for turn-by-turn instructions to work. The Apple Watch's location services may be toggled on and off under the Privacy & Security menu.
- While viewing a list of instructions, tapping the Map button will reveal a map to the location of the next turn. To pan around the map or zoom in and out, use the Digital Crown. Choose "List" to get back to the sequence of events.
- When you've started on your first leg of the journey, your Apple Watch will utilize vibrations and audible cues to tell you when to turn. At an approaching junction, a low tone followed by a high tone (tock tick, tock tick) indicates a right turn, while a high tone followed by a low tone (tick tock, tick tock) indicates a left turn. Having trouble visualizing your final destination? A vibration will let you know when you're in the home stretch and another when you've arrived.

Alerts may be set up for any kind of transportation you like. Choose the notifications you'd want to get from Driving, Driving with CarPlay, Walking, and Cycling in the Apple Watch app on your iPhone by going to My Watch > Maps > Alerts.

The step-by-step navigation is provided by Google Maps. The direction of travel, the distance to the turn, and the name of the street at which the arrow points are all shown. The options to "End", "Map", and "More" may be found at the very end.

The End button, located in the screen's lower left corner, may be used to cancel instructions at any time. Instead, you might choose more, scroll down, and select End.

CHAPTER NINE

HOW TO USE YOUR WATCH TO TAKE CALLS

Respond To A Call

You can see who's calling by raising your wrist when you hear or feel the call alert.

- Press the red Reject button on the call alert to send the call to voicemail.
- To respond using your Apple Watch's built-in microphone and speaker or a Bluetooth-paired device, just tap the Answer button.
- Hit the More buttons, and then pick an option to respond through text message or answer the call using your iPhone. You may put a call on hold until you can answer it on your associated iPhone by tapping Answer on iPhone.

Touch and hold the bottom of the screen, slide up, and then push the Ping Phone button on your Apple Watch to locate your misplaced iPhone.

Name of caller, "Incoming Call," red "Decline" button, green "Answer" button, and more options buttons make up the Apple Watch screen when a call comes in.

During your call

Even if you're on a call that can't be heard over FaceTime, you can transfer it to your iPhone so that you may change the level, dial a number, or use a headset.

- To transfer a call from your Apple Watch to your iPhone, you'll need to unlock your iPhone and hit the green button or bar at the top of the screen while still chatting on your Apple Watch.
  To swiftly put an incoming call on hold, just press your palm on the watch screen for three seconds. Make sure Cover to Mute is on by going to the Apple Watch's Settings menu, selecting

Sounds & Haptics, and then activating the feature.
- Use the Digital Crown to set the desired call volume. If you're on a conference call and don't want to be heard, tap the Mute button.
- To enter more numbers into a call, hit the more icons, then tap Keypad.
- You may transfer the call to an audio device by tapping the More button and selecting one.

When on a FaceTime Audio call, you may change the level, silence the call by selecting the Mute button, or choose a different audio destination by tapping more buttons.

The red Decline button, the Mute button, and the vertical volume indicator all appear when an incoming call is received. Beside the caller's name, the total time of the call is shown.

Check your message inbox

Whenever someone leaves a voicemail, you'll get a notice and may listen by tapping the Listen button there. Access your voicemails on your Apple Watch by opening the Phone app and selecting Voicemail.

You may do the following in the voicemail menu:

- Use the Digital Crown to change the volume.
- Initiate and terminate playback
- You may fast-forward or rewind five seconds
- Message me back
- Do away with the voicemail.

Talk on your Apple Watch

Invoke Siri with a phrase like:

- Just give Max a ring.
- "Dial 555 555 2949"
- "FaceTime audio call to Pete"

Put in a call

1. Launch the Apple Watch's Phone app.
2. Choose "Contacts" from the app list and scroll using the Digital Crown.
3. Choose the desired caller by tapping on them, and then select the phone icon.

4. To make a voice call with FaceTime, either hit the FaceTime Audio icon or enter the phone number.
5. The call volume may be changed by turning the Digital Crown.

A quick way to call someone you've chatted with lately is to go to Recents, and then touch their name. If you have a contact saved as a favorite in the Phone app on your iPhone, you can quickly dial them by tapping Favorites and then dialing their number.

With Watch, you may input a phone number.

1. Switch on your Apple Watch and launch the Phone app.
2. To make a call, choose Keypad, input the number, and then select Call.

During a call, you may utilize the keypad to dial other numbers. Just choose "More," then "Keypad," to use the numeric keypad.

Use Wi-Fi for phone calls.

When your associated iPhone isn't handy or isn't switched on, you may still use your Apple Watch to make and receive calls via Wi-Fi instead of the cellular network, provided that your cellular provider supports this feature. As long as your iPhone is within range of a Wi-Fi network, your Apple Watch will automatically connect.

1. To enable Wi-Fi calling, go to your iPhone's Settings > Phone > Wi-Fi Calling and toggle the switches for Wi-Fi Calling on This iPhone and Add Wi-Fi Calling for Other Devices.
2. Launch the Apple Watch's Phone app.
3. Find the person you want to call and hit the Call button.
4. Choose the contact you want to reach through phone or FaceTime.

Although Wi-Fi may be used to make emergency calls, it is recommended that you utilize your iPhone with a cellular connection whenever feasible. Just turning off Wi-Fi while wearing an Apple Watch will do this.

Apple Watch caller ID functionality

The Apple Watch's Phone app displays caller ID and other details while you're on the go with your iPhone. If you're using headphones or a headset, you may hang up the call from your Apple Watch as well.

Watch With Dual-SIM Capability
Combine the iPhone with the Apple Watch if it has a dual-SIM capability.

You can add additional lines to your Apple Watch with cellular and choose which one to use while connecting to cellular networks if you have an iPhone that supports Dual SIM.

A Watch's cellular functionality is only compatible with iPhones on certain carriers.

Create many different carrier plans

When you initially set up your watch, you will be given the option to add a single plan. The Apple Watch software allows you to add a second plan at a later time.

1. Get out your iPhone and launch the Apple Watch app.
2. Choose Cellular from the My Watch menu.
3. Choose the desired cellular service for your Apple Watch by tapping Setup Cellular or Add a New Plan and then following the on-screen prompts.

Your Apple Watch supports numerous lines, but only one at a time may be active.

Alter your strategies

1. Launch the Apple Watch's Settings menu.
2. Choose Cellular, and then make your selection for the watch's cellular data plan.

To get cellular functionality, launch the Apple Watch app on your iPhone, choose My Watch, and then hit Cellular. The change in your strategy should occur mechanically. If the desired plan doesn't automatically change, touch it.

When utilizing more than one cellular plan, how does the Apple Watch handle incoming calls?

- When an iPhone is paired with an Apple Watch, the wearer may take calls on either line. A badge on your wrist displays the phone number from which the alert was received, such as "H" for "Home" or "W" for "Work." When you answer a call on your watch, it will do so from the line that originally received the call.
- If your Apple Watch is linked to cellular and you don't have your iPhone handy, the phone number you set up in the Apple Watch app will be the one that rings when you get a call. When a call comes in, the Apple Watch software lets you choose which of your lines will be used to make a return call.

If the phone number you've entered into the Apple Watch app is busy when you get a callback, the watch will ask whether you want to use another saved phone number.

Using several carriers with Apple Watch and how messages are received

- Connecting the Watch to an iPhone enables two-way text message delivery. The watch will automatically reply from the line that received the message when you tap the screen.
- If you're away from your iPhone and yet connected to cellular, your Apple Watch may still receive SMS texts on your active plan. When you receive a text message on your Apple Watch, you may answer by sending a message from the same number.
- Although your iPhone is switched off, you may still send and receive messages through your Apple Watch so long as it is linked to a Wi-Fi or cellular network.

Schedule Checks & Edits With Watch

Your Apple Watch displays appointments for the next six weeks and the next two years in the Calendar app (in List and Day view). Your Apple

Watch may display events from any or all of the calendars synced with your iPhone.

An event's specifics are shown on a calendar screen.

Use a question like, "What's my next event?" to Siri.

Examine Watch For Upcoming Events
1. Launch the Apple Watch's Calendar app or choose a date or event from the watch face.
2. Use the Digital Crown to flip through a calendar of forthcoming activities.

The daily schedule is shown on the calendar screen.

3. If you tap an event, you'll be able to view its time, place, attendees, and any associated notes.

A quick touch in the upper left corner will take you to the following function.

Your schedule may be seen monthly or weekly.

Get Moving With Your Device

1. Release the Fitness program. Next, open the Fitness+ app on your iPhone.
   The Fitness app is available in the App Store if you don't already have it.
2. Choose an exercise category (such as Popular or Guest Trainer Series) at the top of the page, and then click through to a specific session.
3. To take any action:

- Incorporate the exercise into My Workouts: Select the Workout to Add option.
- Click the Preview button to get a sneak peek of the exercise routine.

    The workout's accompanying music is also viewable. To listen to the playlist on Apple Music, if you have a subscription, choose Listen in Music.

- To begin the exercise, find the button that initiates it, and then press and hold it until the Play button appears. Select Run or Walk before beginning a Treadmill exercise for the most precise data.

    You may begin the exercise without your Apple Watch, but no data will be recorded from it. To begin your exercise, choose Work Out Without Watch from the menu.

    During a workout, you may broadcast your session to a TV or HomePod that supports AirPlay 2.0 by tapping the screen, tapping the AirPlay button, and then selecting a destination.

Apple TV may also be used to kick off an exercise routine. Find out more about the assignment below.

Additional trainers show you how to modify the routines to make the workout simpler or more difficult. Personal trainers may also guide how to do an activity with less or no external resistance (e.g., using one's body weight).

Adapt Your Perspective

You may toggle between views in the Calendar app by opening it, tapping more icons, and then selecting a different view.

- Next Up: Displays the week ahead of time.
- The happenings for the current day are shown.
- Timeline: Displays everything happening in your life from the last two weeks to the future two years.

If you're in Day view, you can swipe left or right to see the next day; if you're in List view or Up Next view, you can spin the Digital Crown to show the next item.

You may quickly return to the present day and time by tapping the clock in the upper right corner of the screen.

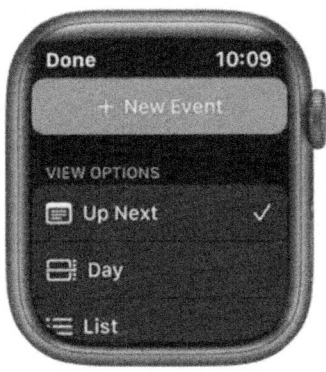

The calendar interface has a "New Event" button up top and Up Next, Day, and List views down below.

Examine Months And Years

You may switch between the week and month views while perusing the calendar in the Day or List view. Launch the Apple Watch's Calendar app and execute one of the following:

- To see the current week, choose the icon () in the upper left corner.
- Go through the weeks by swiping left or right.
- To see the schedule for a certain day of the week, just tap the calendar's week view.
- Display the current month by tapping in the upper left corner when the current week is shown.
- To switch months, just turn the digital crown.

- Touch the week you want to see on the monthly calendar.

Put in a trendy

The Calendar app on your iPhone will automatically sync with your Apple Watch whenever you add an event. The watch itself may be used to schedule things.

- To schedule a FaceTime call with your mother on May 20 at 4 p.m., just tell Siri to "create a calendar event named FaceTime with Mom."
- To create a new event in the Watch's Calendar app, choose the more buttons in the Up Next, Day, or List view. Choose the calendar you'd want to add the event to, give it a name, description, start and finish time, and invitees, and then press Add.

New appointment on the calendar. The event's name appears at the top, followed by a Location

text box. There's an "All-day" option in the footer. There's a button labeled "Start Date" down here.

Modify or remove a scheduled event

- To remove a custom event, select it, hit Delete, and then select it again.
You have the option of canceling just this one occurrence or all of them if this is a series.
- To modify an event, use the iPhone's Calendar app.

React to a request made using Calendar

Apple Watch allows you to quickly and easily react to incoming event invites, either immediately or at a later time.

- Once you get an invitation, you may accept it, decline it, or say maybe by using the buttons at the bottom of the notice.
- If you see the notice hours or days after it was sent, tap it in the list of notifications, scroll, and reply.
- To react to an event while in the Calendar app, just tap on it.

A call, message, email, or Walkie-Talkie button will appear next to the event organizer's name in the event information when you touch on the name.

Find your way to a function.

Your Apple Watch will tell you how to go to an event if you add a location to the invite.

1. Launch the Apple Watch's Calendar application.
2. Choose a gathering, and then select the location.

Modify the "leave now" messages

A "leave now" notification will appear on your Apple Watch depending on the expected journey time and traffic conditions if an event contains a location. Here's how you zero down on a precise window of time, say, two hours before the big show:

1. Launch the iPhone's Calendar application.
2. Listen to the show.
3. Choose the desired time frame from the Alert menu.

Modify your calendar's settings.

Follow these steps to modify the calendar alerts you get and choose which calendars will be shown on your Apple Watch:

1. Get out your iPhone and launch the Watch app.
2. Choose Calendar by selecting My Watch first.
3. Choose Notifications > Calendars > Custom.

Get Your Apple Fitness+ Routine Going

An Apple Fitness+ session may be kicked off on an Apple TV, iPhone, or iPad. The Apple Fitness+ routines are designed to be challenging regardless of your fitness level, so you can use them whether you're just starting or are a seasoned pro. You can start a workout and stop it at any moment; after you're done, you may evaluate it.

Get Moving With An Apple TV Exercise

1. Select the exercisers from the Fitness app.
2. Choose a category of exercise, then a specific routine, to get started.
3. To take any action:
   - The pre-workout briefing: Choose Preview.
   - Kick off your exercise by: If you haven't already joined, start your free trial now, otherwise start your exercise.
   Select Run or Walk before beginning a Treadmill exercise for the most precise data.
   - Start the exercise with some of the Music: To access the workout playlist in the Music app (Apple Music membership needed), scroll down to the list of tracks and tap on a song title.

- To see similar exercises, scroll down to the Related Workouts row and then to the left or right.

An exercise may be interrupted and picked back up at any time.

The Apple Watch or the device playing the exercise may be used to pause it.

- You can accomplish any of the following on the Watch:
    - Pressing the side button and Digital Crown together will pause a workout. Alternatively, you may hit the Pause button after making a left or right swipe.
    - Pressing the side button and the Digital Crown together, swiping right and selecting Resume, or swiping left and selecting Play will resume an exercise routine.
- You can accomplish any of the following on an iOS device:
    - Exercise break: To pause, touch the screen and hold down the finger.
    - To go back to your exercise, just hit the Play button.
- Using Apple TV:

- Workout breaks and restarts: To activate Siri, either press the middle of the clickpad (Siri Remote 2) or the touch surface (Siri Remote 1). The Play/Pause button on the Siri Remote must be pressed.

Summing Up A Workout

The Apple Watch or the device playing the exercise may be used to stop the program.

- Select End with a right swipe on your Apple Watch.
  A breakdown of your exercise is shown. Please choose Done to return to the Workout app.
- If you're using an iOS device, choose End, then End Workout to finish your routine.

  A breakdown of your exercise is shown. To save the routine to My Workouts, use the Add button; to share it; to select a cooldown routine from Mindful Cooldown; or to exit back to Apple Fitness+, select Done.

- To end a workout on Apple TV, use the Menu button on the Siri Remote or Apple TV Remote.

  A breakdown of your exercise is shown. Choose a cooldown exercise by selecting Mindful

Cooldown, or exit to Apple Fitness+ by selecting Done.

The iPhone's Fitness app stores your exercise data so you may review it at a later time.

A class that you have already attended will have a checkmark next to its thumbnail in the list of exercises.

Use Shareplay For A Group Workout

You and up to 32 of your closest friends may get in a workout together with the help of SharePlay Group Workouts. The Fitness app is available on the iPhone, iPad, and Apple TV, and it may be used in conjunction with a FaceTime chat.

When you and your friends are doing HIIT, Treadmill, Cycling, or Rowing workouts together, the workout will play at the same time and everyone can control the playback from their own devices, so you can all motivate each other, see when someone closes an Activity ring, and receive notifications when someone moves ahead of the pack on the Burn Bar.

Using Apple Fitness+ in a group setting calls for the following Apple products: Devices running iOS 15.1

or later are supported, including the iPhone, iPad, and iPod touch. tvOS 15.1 or later is required for playback on Apple TV. Macs need to be running macOS Monterey 12.1 or later for playback. Some nations and locations may not have access to FaceTime or some FaceTime capabilities, and the availability of other Apple services may also vary by country and region. You'll need to be running watchOS 9.1 or later on, an Apple Watch Series 4 or later to utilize it throughout your exercise.

Create A Group Workout On Your iPhone
Create a Group Workout on your iPhone or iPad and kick it off using FaceTime.

1. Initiate a call with FaceTime.
2. Launch the Health & Fitness app on your iOS device. The next step is to open Fitness+ on your iPhone.
   You may get the Fitness app from the App Store if it isn't already installed on your iOS device.
3. Choose a routine, launch it, and then hit SharePlay to get everyone on the call moving at the same time. (If you want the other people on the call to utilize SharePlay and join in the Group Workout, they may need to press Open when requested to do so.)

All listeners to the call will hear the exercise begin at the same time. Those who don't have it are encouraged to sign up for a subscription or try out the service for free (if one is offered).

The exercise may be played and paused using the devices' (including Apple Watches') native playback controls.

Tap the X in the upper left corner of the screen on your iPhone or iPad to cancel an exercise before it's done. Swipe right to dismiss a notification on your Apple Watch.

Launch The Fitness App

Launch the Fitness app on your iOS device, then choose "Group Workout."

1. Launch the Health & Fitness app on your iOS device. The next step is to open Fitness+ on your iPhone.
   You may get the Fitness app from the App Store if it isn't already installed on your iOS device.
2. Just choose a workout, hit "More," then "SharePlay" to broadcast it.
3. Select FaceTime and add the people you want to work out with to the To box.
4. Select Let's Begin after the FaceTime call has connected.

To join in on the exercise, the receiver should hit the workout's title at the top of the FaceTime interface, and then press Open. All listeners to the call will hear the exercise begin at the same time. Those who don't have it are encouraged to sign up for a subscription or try out the service for free (if one is offered).

The exercise may be played and paused using the devices' (including Apple Watches') native playback controls.

Tap the X in the upper left corner of the screen on your iPhone or iPad to cancel an exercise before it's done. Swipe right to dismiss a notification on your Apple Watch.

Participate In A Group Workout

SharePlay on Apple TV allows you to participate in a Group Workout.

The SharePlay buttons won't show up until the same Apple ID is used on both the Apple TV and the iOS device being used for the FaceTime call. Pressing and holding the TV button on the Siri Remote will bring up Apple TV's Control Center, where you may choose a new user or create a new one.

1. Initiate a FaceTime call using an iOS device.

When an active FaceTime call is detected, Apple TV will display a SharePlay indication in the top right corner of the Home Screen.

2. Launch the Fitness app on your Apple TV and choose one of the two options:
- Get your exercise going, then when asked, choose SharePlay and confirm on your iOS device.
- To do this, open Control Center on your iOS device by pressing and holding the TV button on the Siri Remote, then tap the SharePlay button, tap Join, and finally tap Confirm on your iOS device.
3. Find a fitness routine you like and begin it if you haven't previously.

Apple TV and any other devices participating in the FaceTime call play the exercise at the same time. Everyone can control playback in real-time using the controls on their own devices.

Alter The Visuals In Fitness+ Programs

Alter the visuals in Apple Fitness+ programs like meditation and workouts.

Modify The Displayed Statistics

During your routine, your smartphone will provide real-time data on how far along you are in each ring. Wearing an Apple Watch while exercising allows you to monitor your heart rate and calorie expenditure in real-time.

Time, heart rate, and calorie burn data are shown on the screen during an Apple Fitness+ core exercise.

The Burn Bar, included in certain exercises, lets you see how your performance metrics stack up against those of other users who have completed the same activity. The higher up on the Burn Bar you are, the more calories you have burned. In addition to your other stats, the workout report will also record where you landed on the Burn Bar.

During a workout, you may customize the Apple Watch stats that are shown on the screen. The

Fitness app's metrics are synchronized across all of your Apple ID-enabled devices.

Fitness+ members who have an AirPlay-enabled display may now view their exercise data in real-time from their Apple Watches.

1. Select the Metrics option while you're working out.

    Use these motions when exercising with Apple TV:

    - To access the Metrics pane on the second-generation Siri Remote, press down on the click pad ring or slide down on the clickpad.
    - To access the Metrics pane on the first-generation Siri Remote, swipe down to see the Info pane.
2. Pick one of these options:
    - Disable all analytics by clicking the Show Analytics toggle.
    Your data will still be gathered, but it won't be visible.
    - Select "Off," "Show Time Elapsed," or "Show Time Remaining" to alter the time display.
    Powering down Your exercise interval timer will continue to display the current time.

- Stop the Burn Bar by pressing the "Burn Bar" button.

If you disable the Burn Bar, your workouts will not count toward your personal Burn Bar and you will not be able to see your progress after each session.

Feed In Subtitles And Captions

Apple Fitness+ has both regular captions and SDH subtitles for all meditations and exercises. Below the workout's duration, genre, and addition date, you'll notice whether closed captioning and SDH are available.

- To change the language during a workout on an iPhone or iPad, press the More icon, then select Subtitles.
- Depending on the kind of remote you have, you may use Apple TV in one of two ways when working out:
- To choose a language for the subtitles on the second-generation Siri Remote, press down on the click pad ring or swipe down on the click pad to bring up the Info pane.
- For the original Siri Remote, swipe down to see the Info panel, then tap "Subtitles" to choose a language.

Printed in Great Britain
by Amazon